HUGH GIBSON AND A CONTROVERSY OVER POLISH — JEWISH RELATIONS AFTER WORLD WAR I

UNIVERSITAS IAGELLONICA

ACTA SCIENTIARUM LITTERARUMQUE

MXLIII

POLONIA EXTRANEA, FASCICULUS XVI

POLONI ET IUDAEI TEMPORIBUS, QUAE PRIMUM BELLUM MUNDIALE SECUTA SUNT, QUO INTER SE ANIMO FUERINT

Relationes historicas Hugonis
Gibson collegit et praefatione instruxit
ANDREAS KAPISZEWSKI

SUMPTIBUS UNIVERSITATIS IAGELLONICAE

ZESZYTY NAUKOWE
UNIWERSYTETU JAGIELLOŃSKIEGO
MXLIII
PRACE POLONIJNE, ZESZYT 16

HUGH GIBSON AND A CONTROVERSY OVER POLISH — JEWISH RELATIONS AFTER WORLD WAR I

A documentary history compiled
and introduced by
ANDRZEJ KAPISZEWSKI

NAKŁADEM UNIWERSYTETU JAGIELLOŃSKIEGO

REDAKTOR SERII POLONIJNEJ

Hieronim Kubiak

OBWOLUTĘ I OKŁADKĘ PROJEKTOWAŁ

Janusz Bruchnalski

ISBN 83-233-0505-6
ISSN 0137-2416

WYDAWNICTWO I DRUKARNIA
„SECESJA"
Nowy Wiśnicz 327
Zakład w Krakowie, ul. Zakopiańska 62

CONTENTS

PREFACE

In April 1919, Hugh Gibson was appointed the first American Minister to the newly reborn Poland. This became for him most important post in his thirty years of foreign service. Poland was a sensitive and pivotal site for American diplomacy. It was one of the keys to United States policy in post-war Europe, and Washington's immediate involvement in Polish affairs was very significant. Woodrow Wilson was personally committed to Poland's independence. Polish-American volunteers fought in the Polish Eastern territories. The American delegation at the Paris Peace Conference was actively engaged in negotiating a post-war settlement in Poland, including solving the very complicated issues of the country's borders and mediating Poland's conflicts with her neighbors and with the minorities living on her territory. Massive American relief efforts helped to overcome the dire situation in the country caused by long occupation by Russia, Prussia and Austria and the war.

Gibson was well prepared to serve in this post. He had completed a course of instruction at the famous *Ecole Libre des Politiques* in Paris and already had ten years of experience in the foreing service. He had served in the embassies in Belgium, Germany, England and France during the war and traveled with Herbert Hoover on relief missions to many European countries. Hoover strongly recommended him to President Wilson for a promotion:

I cannot speak too highly of his abilities... I have known him under the most difficult of circumstances and he has never failed a representation of the United States in the way all of us would desire, both as to ability, courage and accomplishment. To my knowledge, he has been one of your most ardent and constant supporters.[1]

Gibson did not expect this appointment. In his diary he wrote:

I am still a good deal surprised and a little incredulous about the appointment. I had thought there was some chance of my going to Prague at least temporarily but as Poland is probably the most important legation we now have in view of its relations to Russia and Germany to say nothing of its own special problems I had thought the President would want to send somebody whom he knew well and in whom he had complete confidence.[2]

The president, however, realized the necessity of having highly professional representatives in foreign posts, and Gibson received this nomination as the best qualified candidate.

Gibson was "delighted" with the nomination and "looked forward to it as a great opportunity to do constructive and helpful work".[3] Poles and Polish Americans were gratified with his appointment. The American press wrote a number of approving articles, praising Gibson's previous diplomatic service.[4]

Gibson's appointment to Poland was, from they very first day, difficult for him. One of the most complicated and intractable problems he faced was Polish-Jewish antagonism, which also caused considerable tensions in the Jewish and Polish communities in America and, hence, created domestic political problems for the Wilson administration. Moreover, Polish-Jewish relations became a focus of attention during the final stages of the Paris Peace Conference because of their direct relevance to discussions of the so-called Minorities Treaties, which were intended to protect the Jews and other minorities in Eastern Europe. Gibson played a very important role in shaping up American decisions on those issues. Nevertheless, his reports on Polish-Jewish relations aroused strong criticism from many American Jewish leaders, who accused him of distorting facts and denying the existence of progroms against Jews. This controversy over pogroms in Poland caused Polish Prime Minister Ignacy Paderewski and Herbert Hoover to suggest President Wilson to send a fact-finding mission to Poland. Headed by Henry Morgenthau, it arrived in Poland in July 1919, causing yet another heated controversy in American-Jewish circles. Some Jewish leaders opposed the idea of the mission itself, its composition, and Morgenthau personally; later they rejected the findings of the mission. Gibson supported the mission and criticized actions taken by against it.

Every major work dealing with this period notes the problems which Gibsons' reports caused in America and in Paris. Opinions about them, however, are very divided. Eugene Black, for example, wrote that the reports were "ill-informed", repeated typically anti-Semitic legends "of Jewish pro-Germanism, treachery, espionage, profiteering and bolshevism" and described "all the Jews who were not Assimilants or Chassidim — as 'criminals".[5] He stated that "Gibson's later denials and feeble argument that his reports were garbled in transmission made Gibson doubly foolish and cast doubts on American diplomatic intelligence". Ronald Swerczek, in his Ph. D. dissertation about Gibson's diplomatic career, wrote that "while Gibson did not in theory approve of pogroms or even of harassment of Jews, he did have certain anti-Semitic prejudices which made it difficult for him to understand the apprehensions of Jewish leaders seriously concerned about the welfare of their co-religionists in Poland".[6] He added that Gibson held "a common stereotyped opinion of Jews — that they were frequently sly and conniving, rather than straightforward"; like many other white, Anglo-Saxon, Protestant Americans, "he aired certain prejudices of which he was not even fully aware, so much were they a part of him". On the other hand, Piotr Wandycz believed that Gibson's reports were "fairly objective" as he was not only "unfriendly" to the Jews but "was not an uncritical admirer of Poles either".[7] Kay Lundgreen-Nielsen, in her fundamental book about Polish problems at the Paris Peace Conference, generally agreed with Gibson's findings but avoided making any specific statement about his reports, saying only that they "did not take the direction which the Jewish-led section of American public opinion wished".[8]

None of these histories provides ,however, an in-depth analysis of Gibson's activities or fully discusses the stance of U.S. diplomacy and of American Jewish leaders toward the situation of Polish Jews after World War I. This work is intended to make a contribution to the subject. It presents selections from Gibson's original reports, his official correspondence with the Secretary of State and other U.S. officials. Relevant entries from his private diary are also quoted. Selected documents, representing the points of view of other parties involved, especially the statements and correspondence of American Jewish leaders, are included as well.

These materials help to better understand American actions during the Paris Peace Conference, the politics of American Jewry, and Polish-Jewish relations at that time. This is especially important, as spirited discussions of Polish anti-Semitism, of Jewish attitudes toward the Polish state, and of pogroms, continue to this day, while contradictory popular opinions remain a source of tension between the Polish and Jewish communities in the United States.

The book also partially fills a gap in the record of Gibson's significant role in American diplomacy. So far, almost no books or articles have been devoted to his foreign service (Ronald Swerszek's Ph. D. dissertation on Gibson [1972] was never published, and Perrin Galpin's, *Hugh Gibson. Extracts from his letters and anecdotes from his friends* [1956], is not a scholarly work).

The primary sources for this study were found in the Gibson collection at the Hoover Institution on War, Revolution, and Peace and in the files of the Department of State.

I was able to conduct basic research for this study during my 1989—90 stay in California thanks to the fellowships granted by Stanford University and the Hoover Institution on War, Revolution and Peace. Many people in those institutions helped me in various ways to accomplish my goals. Professors Mark Mancall, Robert Hessen and G. Robert Hamrlda deserve special thanks for reading the manuscript and providing me with a number of valuable remarks. Professor Norman M. Naimark and Dr. Richard Staar helped me to obtain the additional funds necessary to complete the study at Stanford. Many thanks goes to the staff of Overseas Studies Program and the Hoover Archives for all the help granted to me. Professor Adam Walaszek from the Polonia Research Institute at the Jagiellonian University contributed significantly to the final version of the manuscript.

1. DURING THE PARIS PEACE CONFERENCE

World War I was basically over in November 1918; the signing of the armistice with Germany ended the fighting on the Western Front. The war which destroyed great Empires transformed the map of Europe. The victorious Allied powers and the nations that gained independence after long years of occupation faced very difficult decisions about the post-war settlement on the continent. A special role in this process was played by the United States, England and France, whose leaders shared the view that, being responsible for world peace, they were fully empowered to decide not only the future of defeated Germany and Austria but also of other countries, especially those which had no recent experience in self--government. This great power mentality, combined with the scant knowledge they possessed about Eastern Europe, made it especially difficult to solve the very complex problems of setting up new boundaries and determining the status of national minorities.

Poland was a complicated case. The new republic, which Józef Piłsudski led as Chief of State in November 1918, after 123 years of partitions between Russia, Prussia and Austria, had no frontiers, no established territory, no government, no constitution and no international recognition; "it existed, but no one could crearly define its nature or extent".[1] Nevertheless, the future of Poland, the country, lying between Germany and Russia was crucial for the stability of Europe. Both the new Soviet state and a defeated, but not overpowered, Germany resented Poland's resurgence. Moreover, relations between Poland, her neighboring nations and the minorities living on her territory (Jews, Germans, Czechs, Ukrainians, Lithuanians, and Byelorussians) were often characterized by conflict. The tensions lasted for years and sometimes even took the form of military disputes. In 1918—20 the most dramatic events occurred in the "Eastern Territories" (over the possession of the Ukraine and Lithuania). The Polish-Soviet war threatened the very existence of the new Polish state. To complicate the discussions over Poland even further, Poles themselves were divided about the future character of their country. Some followed

Józef Piłsudski, who, making reference to the historical traditions of the Polish Commonwealth, viewed Poland as a multi-national state with a federative structure. Many supported Roman Dmowski and the program of his National Democrats, who propagated the idea of a uni-national state where the supposedly superfluous and trouble making minorities (and especially the Jews) would either become Polonized or emigrate.

Te future of Eastern Europe was also crucial for the Jews living there. The times of tolerant attitudes toward them in the old Polish Commonwealth were over; the end of the nineteenth and the first two decades of the twentieth century were marked, in these territories, where lived the largest Jewish population in the world, by the growth of anti-Semitism. Many Jewish leaders thus saw the Peace Conference as an opportunity to obtain guarantees against oppression and the recognition of Jewish rights as a minority [2]. In an era when ideas of the self-determination of nations were promoted, some Jews started to demand that their group be recognized as a nationality in the modern sense of the term, with all the political and legal consequences such recognition implied. Discussions over this issue were further complicated by the fact that the Jews, like the Poles, disagreed among themselves about most of the questions at hand: they were divided into nationalists, both Zionist and autonomist, and into assimilationist, religiously orthodox, and socialist camps.

All major Jewish bodies sent representatives to the Paris Peace Conference. American Jewry was represented by the delegation of the American Jewish Congress; by a separate, but not separatist, delegation of the American Jewish Committee; and by a small representation of anti-Zionist groups led by Henry Morgenthau. In March 1919, they consolidate themselves and, together with the representatives of the East European Jews, created a Committee of Jewish Delegations at the Paris Peace Conference. The Committee, dominated by moderate Zionists, had as its first two chairmen Julius Mack, one of the leaders of the American Zionist Organization and the American Jewish Congress, and Louis Marshall from the American Jewish Committee. They were replaced in May by Nahum Sokolov, the Zionist who headed the Provisional Jewish National Council of Poland.

The Committee functioned, in practice, as an advocate for East European Jews, whose fate was of deep concern to American Jewry, and to Zionists in particular, not only because of shared ideological and spiritual ties in the Diaspora, but also because the mass of the American Jewish community was of East European origin. The national demands of East European Jews were, however, opposed in Paris by French and British Jewish representatives who believed that Jews should seek recognition for themselves only as a religious minority whose members should be recognized in all other respects as nationals of the country in which they lived. Under pressure from the powerful delegation of American Jews, a compromise was achieved which largely corresponded with the Zionists' minimal demands: guarantees of citizenship and other civil rights, the recognition of Jews as a national entity (with proportional representation in parliament and other state bodies), linguistic autonomy and the right to maintain their own educational, religious and social institutions. The Committee, realizing, that a special status just for the Jews could increase hostility toward them, pressed for the same rights for all national minorities. The Committee members, through memoranda and personal approaches, significantly influenced the U.S. delegates. Even without this influence, most of the American representatives in Paris, and President Wilson himself, fully supported the idea of well-grounded guarantees for the protection of the Jews and other minorities in the newly established states, not only because of the democratic and humanistic ideals they shared but also because they believed that oppression and lawlessness encouraged the spread of Communist ideology. They supported the rights of individuals but were opposed to the idea of "national" rights for the Jews, as they did not want to create precedents, possibly dangerous, for the United States as well.

The Poles, led in Paris by Roman Dmowski and, in the final stages of the Conference, by Prime Minister Ignacy Paderewski, discussed the Jewish issue with various delegates and with the Jewish representatives. Paderewski repeatedly guaranteed the Jews in Poland the same civil rights they enjoyed in the leading western democracies, but he rejected demands to distinguish them from the rest of the population as a national minority. In the end, the Allied Powers decided that rights for the minorities should by guaranteed by special "minorities treaties", to be signed by several East European countries and supervised by the League of Nations. The idea of protecting minorities agreed in principle with Polish traditions; but the procedure was humiliating for Poland. The Poles themselves stipulated that rights for minorities, like all other rights, should be guaranteed by a country's constitution and protected by the state authorities; they did not accept the notion, however, that the exercise of such rights should be supervised by foreign bodies, because this would constitute a limitation of the nation's sovereignty. Moreover, such restrictions were not proposed for all countries, especially not for recently defeated Germany, although it too contained significant minorities within its population. The Polish Parliament eventually ratified the Minorities Treaty but many Poles continued to oppose the very idea of it and accused the Jews of being the cause of this foreign interference in their internal affairs.

The discussions in Paris were not devoid of drama. News about alleged massive pogroms against the Jews began to reach the West toward the end of 1918 and in the Spring of 1919 and was widely publicized by the

Jewish representatives at the Peace Conference. During the discussions over the Minorities Treaties in the middle of May 1919, Julius Mack sent a cable to Jewish organizations in America asking them "to protest in the loudest voice against the pogroms and massacres of the Jews in Poland".[3] Lucien Wolf, a representative of British Jewry, and Louis Marshall discussed this issue as well. Wolf wrote in his diary:

Both Marshall and I received further batches of horrors from Poland today, and we are bombarding our respective Delegations with them. I am afraid it is no good resisting any longer the proposed campaigns against Poland. We are in the presence of what certainly looks like a deliberate attempt to thin out the Jewish population of Poland by massacre, and we cannot stand still, more especially as the Polish Treaty now seems safe enough. Another reason why it seems desirable to denounce these infamies in public is that there is every probability of an early triumph of the anti-Bolshevist forces in Russia, and this is almost certain to be followed by huge butcheries of Jews if we do not make an example of the Poles in good time. The telegrams and other narratives about the pogroms are being given out to the newspapers and Marshall and I discussed plans today for the widest possible publicity.[4]

Protests in the United States, influenced or not by some Jewish delegates at Paris, expanded considerably. Until the Spring of 1919 they were mostly limited to critical articles in Jewish newspapers; in mid-May, however, they took the form of street demonstrations and resolutions sent to President Wilson, to Congress and to the Deparment of State. In big cities Jews organized "days of mourning". Jewish workers went on strike to protest against the events in Poland. Jewish shop-owners decorated their windows in black, and Jewish children were released from schools to participate in demonstrations. Jewish war veterans paraded in their American military uniforms, getting additional sympathy from the public. State governors, city mayors, senators, congressmen and other influential politicians were asked to support the protest actions, and many of them did. The largest demonstrations were organized on May 21. The one in New York City gathered over one hundred thousand Jews.[5] During a meeting in Madison Square Garden, organized under the auspices of the Committee for the Protection of Jewish Rights in Poland and Eastern Europe, Nathan Strauss, a leading Zionist, said, referring to Poland, that „those nations which permit persecution of the Jews will themselves come to an ignominious end, and the quicker that happens the more you and I will be pleased". In turn, Jacob Schiff from the American Jewish Committee urged that "a place in the Leaque of Nations and in the family of free nations should be denied to Poland unless the Polish Government prevented pogroms and granted fair play to Jews".[6] Many American newspapers reported in detail about these events and published articles about anti-Jewish outbreaks in Poland. Some carried paid advertisements, stating that Jews were being "slaughtered", that a wave of pogroms "was sweeping Poland", and that the Jewish people had never been set upon by an enemy "more merciless and brutal".[7]

Poles in the United States denied these reports, seeing them as Jewish propaganda having little to do with reality.[8] At the same time, they perceived Jewish demands in Paris as a deliberate attempt to weaken the Polish position at the Conference, to turn the attention of the delegates from issues much more important to a newly re-born state, and to limit the country's sovereignty and its credibility. John Smulski, the President of the Polish National Department in America, a Polish-American umbrella organization, challenged these accusations in a special statement saying that Poles had been subjected to "abuse and misrepresentation".[9] All major Polish-American organizations protested the Jewish charges and discussed how to counteract and limit the damaging impact of Jewish protests on American public attitudes toward Poland.[10] Not believing what was written in the newspapers, they decided to ask the American government to obtain from Hugh Gibson, newly appointed American Minister in Warsaw an official report about the situation of Jews in Poland and about Polish attitudes and behavior toward them. On May 24, 1919, Kazimierz Żychlinski, the President of the Polish National Alliance, the biggest Polish-American organization, sent a letter on this matter to Jan Kleczka, at that time the only Polish-American representative in the Congress. Żychlinski described the Jewish anti-Polish campaign. He wrote:

You know the latest pronouncements of the Jews related to the supposed pogroms in Poland. This anti-Polish movement acquires all the traits of a racial conflict. Already today, it evokes such an irritation among the Polish workers that it may lead to quite undesired consequences, very destructive for the peace in this country... For instance, in the New York area, the Jews had attacked Poles to such an extent that the latter asked the PNA for protection; in Chicago, the Jewish workers of the tailors' factories, for instance of Hart, Schaffner and Marx, annoyed the Polish workers and on any day the fighting could start.[11]

Żychlinski then asked Kleczka to take the floor in the House and request a report from Ambassador Gibson about pogroms in Poland. He thought that Poles should not fear such a report; on the contrary, it should help defend them against unfounded attacks. Żychlinski hoped that presenting all aspects of Polish-Jewish relations would stop the Jewish propaganda; thus, "it would serve both America and Poland."

On May 26, the New York Times published a front-page article entitled "Jews Massacred, Robbed by Poles" based on reports received in Paris from Jews in Poland. Louis Marshall gave the Times correspondent details of pogroms in Pinsk, Vilna and other places in Western Galicia. On the same day, the Senate passed a resolution introduced by Senator William Calder from New York, stating that "it is reported that innocent men, women, and children, particularly of the Jewish faith, are being outraged and massacred in Poland, Romania and Galicia" and requesting President Wilson to confer in Paris with the representatives of these countries "and to inform them that this body and the American people deeply deplore acts of violence and cruelty".[12] In the following days, probably due to Mack's appeal from Paris, a number of Jewish resolutions protesting against pogroms in Poland were sent to the House and the Senate by different Jewish organizations.[13]

At the same time that Kleczka was energetically working on Capitol Hill [14], the National Defense Committee, another Polish-American umbrella organization, organized a big demonstration in New York on June 2 to protest Jewish actions. Knowing already about the Senate resolution, people at the rally appealed to both chambers of Congress not to undertake any more steps before listening to both sides. They also requested that the President and the Secretary of State take measures to stop what they perceived as an anti-Polish campaign.[15] Similar protest rallies took place in many other cities.

The State Department tried to find out what was really happening in Poland even before the Senate resolution. On April 25, William Phillips, the Acting Secretary of State, cabled Gibson that Jewish leaders had furnished the Department with reports that Jews were massacred by Poles in Pinsk on April 5. He requested Gibson, upon arrival in Poland, "to investigate very carefully truth of matter and report promptly to Department." [16]

Gibson, arrived in Warsaw on April 28, and conducted a preliminary inquiry; he sent a brief cable back to Phillips on May 17 stating that the reports referred to in the Department's telegram were "inaccurate".[17]

On May 21, Frank Polk, then the Acting Secretary of State, at the request of Senator Joseph France of Maryland, sent another telegram to Gibson expressing deep concern about the issue of the alleged pogroms, especially as it had been widely discussed in American newspapers. He wrote that conflicting statements were being issued constantly by Poles and Jews and that it was important for the Department to know "the real truth" at the earliest possible moment.[18]

Two days later Polk informed Gibson about the Jewish gathering in Madison Square Garden and urged him to send Washington a report about the situation, because the issue of pogroms would undoubtedly continue to be raised in America and would be discussed in the Congress. He repeated the request to Gibson to "very fully and promptly" inform the State Department of "the exact truth" concerning the treatment the Jews received from Poles, including the question of religious toleration and the attitudes of the Jews towards the Poles.[19]

On May 26, in Paris, Louis Marshall handed President Wilson the texts of the speeches and resolutions of the Madison Square Garden meeting and press clips from American newspapers on pogroms in Poland.[20] By May 28 Polk had not yet received any report from Gibson and he cabled him again, informing him that American newspapers were

publishing long articles giving dates and places where Jews were reported to have been massacred or otherwise mistreated. Congressman Isaac
Siegel had personally furnished the State Department with another such
list. Polk than requested Gibson to give his investigation a priority over
other matters.[21]

Gibson, lacking staff and just beginning to organize the Legation, was
not very happy about the time consuming requests coming from Washington, which took him away from duties he considered more important at the moment. Moreover, he thought that exaggerated reports about
outbreaks against the Jews should not receive so much attention in America. He wrote in his diary:

We are in the midst of turmoil. We are getting telegrams every day from America
about alleged massacres of Jews in Poland and instruction to report. It means a lot
of telegraphing to explain the situation. If there were massacres it would be easier
to handle for there would be something to report but it is hard to explain things that
do not happen. There were some Jews killed early in April at Pinsk, a town in the
eastern districts occupied by the Polish army. The Jews form more than half of the
population. They were outspokenly hostile to the Polish Government and laid themselves open to suspicion. One evening when it was touch and go whether the town
would be taken back by the Bolsheviki the Jews held a meeting under very suspicious
circumstances. After it had been raided a number of the men were taken out and
shot. It was certainly summary justice such as likely to be meted out on all fronts,
and the officer responsible may have assumed too much authority. The Polish Government felt that he had and removed him the next day. But the fact was in the
fire and Jews all over the world have been excited about the matter ever since.
I have never seen a matter concerning which so many versions were issued. I get
a new one every day. An inter-allied mission was sent to the place immediately and
made a thorough investigation on the ground, examining witnesses, etc. There is no
doubt that the Jews were killed there is also no doubt that their behaivor was such
as to invite trouble. It was in no sense a religious matter. However official reports
are powerless to quiet the propaganda artists and they are getting stronger and
stronger every day. Now they are manufacturing massacres of Jews at all sorts of
places and sending cables about the need for our saving the lives of all sorts of Jews
who are very much surprised when we ask about them to know that they have been
considered in danger. There is a big propaganda bureau at Kowno, not far from Vilna,
now in German occupation and its main function is to send out long reports of the
killing of Jews in Poland, regardless of fact. The Berlin papers carry these yarns
and they get into the neutral papers and gradually into our own. Of course it is to
the advantage of the Germans to stir up as much dissention in Poland as possible
so as to keep the country weakened. There are other influences with similar interests
and altogether I can see that we are in for a long siege of Jewish atrocities. I am
gathering all facts I can so as to be ready to send it in when the need comes but I am
desperately crippled by lack of staff. It needs a crowd of judicial minded men to do
nothing but try to investigate this one question.[22]

On May 30 Gibson sent his first report to Washington. He stated that
he used all possible sources of information to reconstruct the events: the
representatives of American organizations operating in Poland (the
American Relief Administration, the American Red Cross), of Allied

missions in the country, and of the American Legation (sent especially to Eastern Galicia for that purpose), as well as a number of Jews (including the representatives of the American Joint Distribution Committee) and Polish and Jewish press reports. Gibson wrote:

I have received no reports of atrocities perpetrated against Jews in Poland, Galicia, Lithuania with the exception of the Pinsk and Vilna affairs... There is a bitter feeling against classes of Jews which arises largely from economic causes and not from religious intolerance. This gives rise to a considerable amount of petty persecution which cannot be prevented or readily controlled by Governmental action. Certain elements of the Jews support the Government and are respected as an integral part of Polish nation. Another large element of the Jews are outspokenly and avowedly hostile to the Government and this attitude has served to intensify bad feeling.[23]

Gibson next presented in detail the events of April 20 in Vilna where, during figthing between the Polish and Soviet armies, a number of people were killed. Several foreign representatives investigated the incident, along with the members of the Jewish Joint Distribution Committee and other American organizations, and they were, according to Gibson, "unanimous in reporting that there was no Jewish massacre in that city; this was confirmed by the statements in the Jewish press in Warsaw". [24] On the same day, May 30, he also sent the State Department another cable asking for specific information about the alleged pogroms which could help him with the investigation. Understanding the importance and sensitivity of the issue, Gibson asked Washington to approve his personal undertaking of the investigation on the spot in those places where outbreaks occurred and asked to be accompanied by some reliable American non-governmental observers. He wrote:

Since my arrival in Poland I have endeavored to inform myself fully as to the treatment of Jews but possess no evidence which would warrant charges referred to in Department's telegram or afford me any data to start specific investigations, therefore I should be glad to have Department furnish me a definite list of places where these events occurred, a statement of the charges made, the events in each place and if possible names of victims and of possible witnesses. If Department approves, I am then prepared to ask Doctor Bogen, director of the Jewish Joint Distribution Committee for Poland, and Lieutenant Colonel Bailey of the Red Cross to accompany me and make careful personal investigation in the various places.[25]

Gibson, again displaying his disapproval of the behavior of some Jews, wrote in these days in his diary that "our Jewish friends come dashing in and tell us every time they hear of anybody who made a face at a Jew and even the Jewish newspapers have on word of pogroms though they lambaste the Poles day in and day out and curse them for every crime in the calendar".[26] According to Gibson, all the reports about pogroms were "exclusively of foreign manufacture for anti-Polish purposes".[27]

On May 31 Gibson cabled Washington a report of a Lieutenant Foster, who was sent to Pinsk to investigate the pogrom which allegedly took place there on April 5. According to Foster, the Polish commander of the city, which was surrounded at the time by the Soviet army, received information from two Jewish soldiers under his command that Zionist Jews were organizing a meeting to prepare an anti-Polish, pro-Soviet uprising. In the situation, he arrested those attending the gathering and shot 35 of those who thought were Communists. Foster reported:

It is my opinion and the opinion of the British and French officers who accompanied me that this shooting cannot be considered in any way as pogrom or anti-Jewish aspect massacre. Our conversation with the representative Jews of Pinsk brought out the fact that there existed in Pinsk a disturbing element of younger Jews radical in sentiment who opposed all efforts Jewish or otherwise to better conditions in the town and it was this element that created the difficulties at the meeting ... I may add that the Polish military authorities welcomed our investigation, placed existing facilities at our disposal and interfered in no way with our examination of witnesses by only the English officer and myself. There was no Pole present and the entire examination was carried on under the direction of the principal Jewish rabbis of Pinsk who furnished interpreters when such were necessary.[28]

On the same day Gibson discussed Polish-Jewish relations with Józef Piłsudski, the Polish Chief of State. They talked, in particular, about the outbreaks in Częstochowa on May 27, described in the American press as another pogrom. Gibson wrote that Piłsudski had given positive instructions to the Polish Army that he would not tolerate anti-Jewish acts, that punishment would be severe and that the officers were to be held responsible for the behavior of their men. Piłsudski also sent his Minister of the Interior to Częstochowa to investigate the incident on the spot. Gibson reported:

General Piłsudski was evidently alarmed and indignant. He said that to persecute the Jews brought shame upon the name of Poland and could not but harm the country, that no matter what might be said these millions of Jews are in Poland; they are not going to leave Poland and the Poles have got to live in close contact with them. 'The Government as well as all good Poles are strongly opposed to any persecution for we know that we cannot settle down to peaceful development while there is discord among elements of our own population. For the good of the country the Government is determined to put down any anti-Jewish activites with an iron hand'.

Confidential. He told me that until the last few days he had felt that anti-Jewish persecution pretty well at an end but that the troops newly arrived from France [i.e. General Haller's army composed, among others, of volunteer Polish-Americans] had shown a disposition to make life miserable for the Jews, chasing them through the streets, cutting off their beards et cetera. That this was causing a recrudescence of such acts by the civil population and this is confirmed by statements made to me this afternoon by reliable American-Jewish informant before I saw General Piłsudski.[29]

On June 1 Gibson cabled the State Department a report written by Frederic Dolbeare, a Secretary of the American Legation in Warsaw, who went to investigate the events in Częstochowa. Dolbeare reported that on May 27 some shots were fired at Silesian soldier. As the Poles accused the Jews of this, a mob went to the Jewish quarter in the city, instigating outbreaks of violence in which several people were killed and many injured. Eventually the Polish army restored order and the man who led the mob was convicted.[30] Gibson telegraphed:

Dolbeare and his colleagues convinced that conditions arose through economic difficulties involved. I learned from relief heads that Chestokhov [Częstochowa] is famous for smuggling of food supplies into Germany, that the Jews have been very active in this work and a number of them have been caught bearing regular licenses from the Germans for smuggling. Food is scarce and prices are high. There is rough element in the population of this district which with hunger and lack of work are for the present out of hand. Dolbeare states that loyal authorities seem to have handled situation well and so as not to arouse the population. They regard the affair as sporadic and do not look for further trouble, provided they can get some food.[31]

On June 2 Gibson sent the State Department a long report with his opinions on the situation of the Jews in Poland.[32] [Document No. 1] First, he characterized different groups of Jews: the pro-Polish assimilators; the orthodox, indifferent to the Polish state; the so called Litwaks, deported from Russia "and openly hostile to Poles"; and the criminals, "like the gun men in New Jork". Next, Gibson expressed his opinion on the major causes of Polish-Jewish tension. According to him, many Polish Jews looked upon their religion as a nationality and their attitude toward the Poles was often "hostile and provocative". The performance of the Jewish press and Jewish members of the Diet only intensified this feeling as they supposedly tried to coerce Poland through the influence of foreign Jews upon their governments. Jews were continually working as spies for the Bolsheviks, the Ukrainians and Germans and acted against the Polish army. Poland's economy was monopolized by Jews, who carried on business by methods "that would not be tolerated in the United States". Moreover, Jews were smuggling food out of starving Poland for profit. All of these factors were causing conflicts. For Gibson, they had, however, no religious tinge and were usually wrongly presented in the West. He wrote that "when a Jew was injured it was called a pogrom" but "when a Christian was mobbed it was called a food riot". He also repeated his earlier findings about the German news agency in Kowno (Kovno, Kaunas) which had been spreading false information about Polish behavior toward the Jews to create tensions within the country and weaken it as a possible rival and enemy.

In the same report Gibson suggested a number of actions to improve the situation; to influence the Polish and Jewish press to moderate their tone; to call assimilated Jews to assist the Polish government more; to invite Polish representatives to visit America to change the incorrect perception of many Poles that the United States was an advocate of the Jews and acted against Poland[33]; to have the State Department discourage violent Jewish anti-Polish agitation based upon "exaggerated or unfounded reports"; to send to Poland some American Jews "who could face facts honestly"; and to refuse passports "to agitators of any sorts". Admitting that the problem required patience and good will on both sides, Gibson praised the Polish government, which, he said, had been "well intentioned" and "amenable to suggestions" although it lacked power and experience in authority.

At that time congressional representatives from New York City, Isaac Siegel, Fiorello La Guardia and Henry Goldfogle, separately introduced in the House drafts of three resolutions bitterly assailing Poland for massacres of Jews.[34] During the hearings on this issue in the House Foreign Affairs Committee, Congressman Kleczka, in turn, defended the Poles asserting that news about pogroms was "of German origin designed to show that Poland was incapable of self-government". Assistant Secretary of State William Phillips presented the latest reports from Gibson, stating that news about outbreaks against the Jews was much exaggerated.

In the meantime the State Department accepted Gibson's request to include other American and Jewish representatives in the investigation of outbreaks. It asked for a new report within a week, telling Gibson that the newspaper reports regarding alleged pogroms had laid special stress on occurrences at Pinsk, Vilna, and Lvov [Lemberg], and that the Department was particularly interested in events which had occurred since the establishment of a responsible Polish Government.[35]

Before leaving Warsaw to conduct the investigation, Gibson sent the Acting Secretary of State his general opinion about the situation in Poland.

Feel I should point out that we may expect disorders with increasing frequency in Poland in the near future. This will largely be from the nervousness of the population due to the following causes:
1. Shortage of the food supply which will continue for some time.
2. Uncertainty over determination of frontiers.
3. Fear of German hostilities.
4. Great extent of unemployment.
These disorders may as a rule be expected to take an anti-Jewish character for the following reasons:
1. Food hoarding and profiteering by certain elements of the Jews.
2. Rumored hostile Jewish influence against Poland in England, France and America and anti-Polish agitation in these countries over Jewish matters.
3. Proposed special treaty for the protection of the rights of minorities which is resented as needlessly imposing on the Polish state conditions most of which would have been adopted without pressure.
4. Relations of Polish Jews with the Germans.
5. Inclination of mobs to pillage food shops which are largely in the hands of the Jews.[36]

In Washington, the House Committee on Foreign Affairs scheduled hearings on the issue of pogroms for June 10. A number of Polish and Jewish leaders were asked to testify. Nevertheless, Stephen Porter,

Chairman of the Committee, decided to put off hearings until Gibson sent a full report about alleged outrages in Poland. Porter told Poles and Jews who came to Washington that he hoped that after Gibson's investigation any further action by the House would be unnecessary, because much news about pogroms was probably only German propaganda to discredit Poles.[37] He also asked representatives of both communities not to mount any public protests around the country until Gibson's report was available. Phillips described this meeting in a letter to Gibson:

The Committee on Foreign Affairs had set a certain date on which they were to receive publicly the testimony of both Poles and Jews regarded the alleged 'pogroms'. The Committee invited me to go to the Capitol and to give them whatever information I could before the public hearings began. As I passed through the Committee's anti-chamber I was startled to find it packed full of 'ruffians', both Poles and Jews, all reday to give their individual testimony. The Committee heard your reports first and promptly decided to cancel the public hearing, with the result that all the 'ruffians' were shipped home without being given a chance to state their case. The Chairman, however, invited them into the room in a body, read them a lecture of the importance of shutting-up and attending to their own business, and dismissed them curtly. From that moment public gatherings of protest in this country began to cease and until now they are a thing of the past. Your reports, therefore, have done a very valuable work for they have materially helped to stop the public meetings which might have been the centers of serious local riots.[38]

In another letter on this matter Phillips wrote Gibson:

It is appalling the amount of antagonism against the Poles which has been deliberately created during the last month by the Jews in this country. The Senate has already passed a resolution and the House is still considering it, censuring severely the Polish Government. I think I was largely instrumental in holding up this resolution in the House by appearing twice before the Foreign Affairs Committee and reading some of your dispatches, which fortunately came in the nick of time.[39]

The situation, however, did not calm down. On June 10 the *New York Times* reported that Louis Marshall received in Paris a "detailed circumstantial account" of the atrocities committed by Poles against Jews in the city of Vilna, a report "of murders, torturing, robberies, and separation of families, giving names and addresses of the victims". Marshall planned to hand this report to President Wilson.[40] Acting Secretary of State Polk immediately cabled Gibson:

Report tells first of disappearance of 400 Jews driven from their homes without leaving traces of their whereabouts. Not until May 7, more than 14 days after they had been sent away, was permission given to Commission to search for these lost people. Report continues 'of the whole party all we know is that they were seen thrown into the cars in a frightful condition and were beaten and robbed.' Report states that the number of killed already totals 60. States further that L. Jaffe, President of the Lithuanian Zionist Association, member of Executive Committee of Jewish Community of Vilna, suffered special mishandling. According to report Israel Benski was shot in his home and his wife and child shot over his dead body, and that Reisa Stein was killed because she protested against arrest of her husband. It is said that under threat of shooting, about 200 Jews were kept in the Theater Platz all day during the 22nd of April and were beaten with the bats of guns, that Chaio Warnian was robbed and tied to the horse of a legionary driven at gallop through the city, that three old men, Aronozicz, Katz and Rabbi Chodes were robbed of everything they had, that about 20 legionaries kept a man named Lichtenstein before a firing squad and demanded 10,000 rubles and that under pretense of a search legionaries and militia plundered shops, warehouses, charitable institutions and synagogues. Report is represented as a flat contradiction of statement of Premier Paderewski that there was no persecution of Jews by Poles.[41]

Gibson went to Vilna to investigate the incident. When he returned to Warsaw on June 15, he immediately responded to Polk's cable, denying most of the information about the persecution of Jews:

Without waiting for general report which is now being prepared I hastened to answer this so to allay the apprehension of individuals in the United States over the reports printed in the *New York Times* as to anti-Jewish excesses in Vilna. The representatives of the Jewish community made no mention of any number of Jews who had been driven away without giving any trace of their whereabouts. A large numebr of people were arrested at time of the occupation of the town and sent to Lida and Białystok so that for some days their whereabouts may have been unknown. These people however have been returned to Vilna and so far as I was able to learn there are none unaccounted for. Jaffe ... suffered no mistreatment according to his own statement. He was arrested, kept with a number of other people at the railroad station and sent to Lida being in custody altogether for six days. He does not claim to have been mistreated during this time. Concerning other people mentioned by name in the Department telegram I have no special information but shall endeavor secure it. Rabbis Rubenstein and Schabe were not beaten or otherwise mishandled although they were both arrested the first day, being released as soon as their identity could be brought to the attention of the military authorities. I talked with both of them alone and at length. As a whole the report in the *Times* appears to be exaggerated.[42]

Gibson made similar remarks in his diary. He wrote that he talked with Jews who were reported as having had "a particularly bad time" and that they "did not give any impression of the cruelty which the newspapers accounts had conveyed".[43]

Meanwhile Gibson cabled Washington a report prepared by Lieutenant Foster, who had gone to Cracow to investigate the events which took place there on June 6.[44] He stated that "one Christian woman and one Jewish boy were killed ... about 100 injured, including police, Christians and Jews ... several Christian shops as were as Jewish [were] pillaged". Gibson suggested that the reasons for Polish-Jewish clashes were "Bolshevik and German agitators, the presence of whom, with high prices and general unemployment of rough laboring elements, creates a difficult situation which is easily upset".

Gibson also sent Washington a protest from Jewish representatives of the communities and political parties from the town of Borysław, Tusta-nowice and Wolanka "against exaggerated charges on the subject of pogroms spread by elements hostile to the Polish army". These protests were submitted to the American Legation by the Polish Ministry of Foreign Affairs.[45]

The content of some of Gibson's reports now became known to American Jewish leaders. They were especially offended by Gibson's classification of some Jews as the "criminal class". Cyrus Adler, of the American Jewish Committee, wrote to the representative of the Joint Distribution Committee in Poland: "Such a characterization is, of course, in itself an indication of ... hostility since no one would ever think of marking any section of a people as a criminal section".[46] On June 14 Louis Marshall issued in Paris a special statement accusing Gibson of distortion of facts.

To one familiar with Polish affairs the report attributed to Mr. Gibson minimizing the extent of the Polish pogroms, is astounding. He has apparently spoken out of the fullness of his ignorance. Until he arrived in Warsaw in the latter part of April there had been no American Legation there. He had no previous knowledge of Polish conditions. As late as a fortnight ago he stated officially that he had made no personal investigation into the subject of pogroms and could not speak authoritatively concerning them. Until June 11 he had made no effort to give them personal attention. On that day he started a tour of inspection to Vilna. Hence his report is necessarily based on the merest hearsay, parrot-like repetition of what has been told him in court circles within whose sacred precincts Jews are not permitted to enter. There, in the face of continuous and unparalleled atrocities that have shocked the civilized world, all the charges met with the stereotyped remark: 'There have never been any pogroms in Poland'. This is usually followed by a pronouncement, the inconsistency and falsehood of which does not abash its authors, that, after all, the victims are Bolsheviki or capitalistic exploiters. Mr. Gibson finds it convenient to disregard conceded facts. He forgets that during the last seven years, at the instance of a political cabal, a pernicious boycott has been waged against Jews, which threatens their destruction industrially and economically.[47]

Next, Marshall challenged Gibson's findings about a pogrom in Pinsk.[48]

He coolly ignores the awful story of Pinsk, where thirty-seven defenseless men were without resistance taken into custody, while engaged in work of philanthropy, by the military authorities, and without the semblance of a trial or hearing were deliberately murdered at the command of a Polish officer, who thus far has not even received a reprimand. He does not seem to know that Paderewski has even expressed qualified regret that some innocent blood was shed on that occasion. He does not appear to have read the official report of Lieutenant Foster of the American Peace Mission, whose findings of fact corroborate the charge of murder. He takes no account of the brutal castigations inflicted on men and women who were imprisoned after witnessing the execution of those near and dear to them and were later discharged as innocent of all wrong. He probably has never heard of the report of Brailsford, the distinguished English publicist, which is in the official files here, who shows that several weeks before the Pinsk murders the very officer who directed the butchery expressed to him his hatred of Jews and declared that one Jew in every ten should be killed. He makes no note of the arbitrary fine of 100,000 marks inflicted after this massacre upon the Jewish population of Pinsk, followed by similar fines in other towns. He regards as unimportant the confiscation by Polish authorities at Pinsk of 1,000,000 marks sent there by the American Jewish relief committees to relieve their brethren dying from famine and typhus, which has as yet been unable to wrest from the hands of the despoiler.

Marshall similarly criticized Gibson's reports about outbreaks in Vilna, Lida, Częstochowa, Cracow, and Lvov.

He is silent respecting the horrors of Vilna, the details of which have been officially reported, with the names of sixty Jews done to death, particulars of property valued at 1,000,000 rubles pillaged and destroyed, a minute narrative of flaggings and other indignities inflicted and of wholesale deportations of hundreds of reputable citizens, who are still undergoing incarceration far from their homes. He seems to know nothing of the occurrences at Lida and many other towns. Nor does he appear to realize what happened at Szenstockau [Częstochowa], although leading Polish journals, avowedly anti-Semitic, have confessed the happening there of a pogrom where at least five Jews were killed and upward of forty seriously wounded. He has failed, so far as the public knows, to report what has just been learned of the attack made upon Jews at Cracow, in which Polish General Staff concedes that soldiers participated, which resulted in the serious wounding of sixty-six Jews and in the infliction of slighter injuries on more than a hundred. He seems to have closed his eyes to the indiscriminate beating and flogging of Jews and to the systematic and diabolical tortures now inflicted upon them. A new kind of sport consists in tearing out by the roots of the beards with the adherent flesh, of Jews in streets, public places, railroad stations, and railway trains, or, by way of variety, severing them with knives and bayonets and setting fire to them. He has deafened his ears to the wails of the anguished Jews in Vilna, who are not even permitted to buy food for their famished children. The story of Lemberg [Lvov] for months has been published, giving the testimony of trustworthy eye--witnesses to the medieval fiendishness with which the Jews were treated. Depositions of what has occurred in many other localities are available.

Finally, Marshall accused Gibson of denying that even the Polish authorities themselves recognized that anti-Semitic outbreaks had taken place.

The Pinsk affair has been made the subject of Parliamentary inquiry, yet Mr. Gibson with profound insouciance either disregards these channels of information or looks upon them as fictitious or negligible. Yet when two aged rabbis, whose membership in the Polish diet and whose venerable appearance and learning did not save them from the gentle dalliance of the brutal mob in the very capitol of Poland, complained of this outrage General Pilsudski, recognizing conditions which do not appear to have come within Mr. Gibson's ken, issued a decree in which he deplored the existence of the disgraceful incidents which Mr. Gibson, more royalist than the king, seeks to deny. And now, concurrently with the application of the coat of whitewash by which our representative seeks to hide the sea of blood that has been and continues to be shed, comes, a special military order from General Haller, the Polish Commander ... in which he admits the truth of complaints of persecutions made by Jews and declares that to strike and wound defenseless people, to inflict cruelties upon them and to despoil them of their property is conduct unworthy of Polish soldiers in the service of a sacred cause.

Marshall's statement became widely known because the *New York Times* printed it on June 17, and it was picked up by many other newspapers. When Gibson learned about that he sent Polk a cable intended to show his influence on the Polish government in improving the situation of Jews in the country:

Since our arrival here we have devoted most of our efforts to Jewish questions. We have discussed the matter at length with Jews of varying opinions and with Poles, both in and out of the Government. I feel that we have been successful in impressing the Government with the seriousness of the situation and they have already acted upon some of our suggestions. The friendly declarations of General Haller and the Minister of the Interior and Governmental pressure enable the press to modify its tone. They realize the friendly spirit which prompts our interest, show a readiness to follow our advice and I believe that other steps will be taken soon. The various excesses, which have taken place since last November, appear to be due chiefly to abnormal conditions. I attach greater importance to the state of public opinion which is undoubtedly bad and may have serious consequences. We are trying to improve the situation in this respect by exterting our friendly influence with Polish Government to adopt obvious measures such as moderating tone of press, controlling actions of troops, issuing strict instructions to officials throughout the country etc. I shall be glad to receive any suggestions as to specific action that the Department may be disposed to offer either as its own views or those of people interested in the question.

Given the increased agitation about pogroms in Poland, Polish-American newspapers published many accounts of people returning from Poland and denying such occurrences.[49] Polish-Americans and their organizations, trying to reach the English-speaking public, published several books, articles, and leaflets defending Poles and accusing Jews of anti-Polonism.[50] The broadest audience was reached by "an open letter" to Nathan Strauss published by Jakub Vorzimer, a Polish-American editor in New York, which was accompanied by fragments of Gibson's reports.[51]

On June 17, Gibson sent Washington a detailed report regarding the events in Vilna prepared together with Boris Bogen and Walter Bailey.[52] [Document No. 2] After discussions in Vilna with the local authorities and representatives of the Jewish community, they described the situation in the city but stated that because of the lack of any contempo_rary record they doubted whether the exact truth about events could ever be ascertained. According to them, the outbreak took place during the fighting between Polish and Soviet troops, before the Polish authorities had obtained control of the city. They reported that at that time there was a widespread feeling among the local Polish population and the Polish soldiers against Jews who were "believed to be allies of the Bolsheviki, war profiteers and enemies to Poland". On entering Vilna, Polish troops were fired on from private houses some of which were occupied by Jews. Searches disclosed fuses, machine guns, and other weapons. On those grounds the Polish military made wholesale arrests, ransacked dwellings and shops, and "summarily" executed a number of persons. After three days the military and civil authorities issued orders against looting and took effective control. No cases of serious violence were reported after that.

As the House Committee on Foreign Affairs was waiting for a final report about the outbreaks before acting on resolutions, the State

Department asked Gibson to complete the investigation and to report specifically whether Bogen from the Jewish Joint Distribution Committee concurred with his conclusions.[53]

This request reached Gibson upon his arriving in Paris, where he had been summoned to assist with the final deliberations of the Peace Conference. He responded by repeating that the report already sent on the Vilna affair was jointly prepared by Bogen, Bailey and himself. The full report about all the outbreaks was to be written by Bogen and Bailey in Warsaw and cabled to Paris, whence Gibson would sent it on to Washington.[54]

Polk, after receiving Gibson's explanation and being reassured about the accuracy of his report, wrote at the request of the President a formal response to the Senate's resolution of May 26. He informed the Senate that Gibson along with Bogen and Bailey, was carrying out the investigation of the charges which had been made that the President "has given some thought to the advisability of sending another commission to Poland, which matter will probably be definitely decided after Mr. Gibson has had an opportunity of discussing the subject at Paris".[55]

In Paris, Gibson fully realized the extent of the criticism his reports had created within parts of the American Jewish leadership, although he hoped for a while that the whole controversy was just a misunderstanding caused by some incorrect report written by somebody else and wrongly attributed to him. He described this situation in a letter he wrote to Dolbeare:

The Jewish situation I found is even more of a ferment than I had anticipated. It seems that the Department gave to the Committee on Foreign Affairs extracts from some of our telegrams. The Committee in turn gave some extracts of these extracts out and the newspapers printed some extracts of these extracts. By that time father could hardly recognize the child. Incidentally our friend, Colonel Godson, seems to have come in with a boob telegram denying that there had been any excesses in Poland. Somebody, either here in the Mission or in Washington, gave that out as coming from me. Upon reading this Mr. Louis Marshall went up in a baloon where he has since remained showering upon me all sorts of invective which is being cabled to New York to keep the situation stirred up ... All the leading Jews in America went to that bat on the subject an have stirred up a lot of feeling.[56]

In one of his daily letters to his mother, Gibson wrote in an even more direct way:

As you may have seen by the papers some damphool gave out a statement made by somebody else as coming from me to the effect that there had been nothing of the nature of pogroms in Poland. All the Jews rose up and smote me hip and thigh and one of the most virulent of them was Louis Marshall who shot off a column to the *New York Times* which sounded by Cicero's denunciation of Cataline.[57]

The situation was tense and required action. It was essential for the American delegation to the Peace Conference to find out how the Jews learned about Gibson's confidential reports and precisely which reports they had obtained. Robert Lansing, the Secretary of State, cabled then to Washington:

Please cable exact texts of those portions of Gibson's telegrams on the Jewish situation in Poland published by Department or House of Representatives. For your confidential information. Considerable embarrassment is being caused Gibson by such publication of extracts from his telegrams instead of in the form of an official statement prepared by the Department. Judge Brandeis and Felix Frankfurter in conversation with Gibson yesterday, intimated that the confirmation of his appointment by the Senate might be jeopardized by the nature of this reports which they stated had done great harm to the Jewish race.[58]

Phillips told Lansing that the State Department had given some statements to the press based on Gibson's reports and that the same had been done by the Chairman of the Congressional Foreign Relations Committee. The statement of June 3 declared that the Provisional Government of Poland had given the American Legation in Warsaw positive assurances that it was opposed to anti-Jewish activities, would not tolerate persecution of Jews in the country, and would take strong measures immediately to protect all Jews in Poland.[59] It also reported Gibson's talk with Piłsudski in detail. The press release of June 7 stated that Gibson, after investigating the issue and talking with members of Jewish community as well as with members of different American missions in Poland, had received no reports of atrocities against Jews in Poland with the exception of the incidents at Vilna and Pinsk. Moreover, reports from different independent sources and from Jewish newspapers in Warsaw "were unanimous that there was no Jewish massacre in Vilna". The statement continued that in Poland "there was feeling against certain classes of Jews largely due to economic reasons rather than to religious intolerance, that certain Jewish elements supported the Government and were regarded with respect as an integral part of the nation of Poland while another Jewish element was openly hostiile to the Government".[60] The second statement obviously quite differed in content and tone from all Jewish reports appearing in American newspapers.

The State Department also showed Gibson's dispatches to Abram Elkus, former American Ambassador to Turkey, in order to obtain his opinion on the issue; he was a respected diplomat and a well known Jew Polk described what happened in his cable to Lansing:

Department has shown Mr. Elkus all of Gibson's reports. Elkus in turn has shown these reports to Messrs. Schiff, Judge Magrader, Rosen, Walcott, Mossburg, Strauss and Stephenwise. Elkus advises that all these persons are entirely satisfied with rulings of the Department and have a feeling of the utmost confidence in Gibson himself. He says there has been some criticism of Gibson, however, because of the publication in the press of a confidential report by the Military Attache at Paris to the effect that no pogroms with our knowledge had taken place in Poland. This statement, they say,

Peace Commission wrongly attributed to Gibson. He thinks that Louis Marshall's attacks upon the American Legation in Warsaw have been made in the belief that the Military Attache's statement was in fact Gibson's. Elkus and his associates have cabled today to Marshall explaining the situation, and affirming their own confidence in Gibson. Elkus suggests that Marshall might be permitted to see the Gibson cable reports which they feel confident will satisfy him as to the Legation's just and fair attitude in the whole matter.[61]

In Paris, Gibson had an opportunity to exchange opinions on the matter with the Jewish representatives there and especially with Marshall. The talks, however, did not diminish the differences in their opinions. Nor was Marshall's position influenced by Elkus cable. Gibson described his meetings with the Jews in Paris in a letter he sent to Dolbeare in Warsaw:

The evening of my arrival [in Paris] I went up to see Colonel House and found Justice Brandeis and Felix Frankfurter, the hot dog of war, there. The Colonel nimbly slipped out of the room and left me to defend myself. These two opened the prosecution by saying that I had done more mischief to the Jewish race than anyone who had lived in the last century. I inquired to know just how that happened. They said that I was known in the United States as a fair-minded and humanitarian citizen and when I put my name to a document it carried weight, that my reports on the Jewish question had gone round the world and had undone their work for months. I still persisted in asking what they objected to and they finally said that I had stated that the stories of excesses against the Jews were exaggerated to which I replied that they certainly were and I should think any Jew would be glad to know it. They further said that I had 'branded the whole Jewish race as gunmen' and that phrase had stuck in the public mind. I gently pointed out that what I had done was to say that there was a small class of renegade Jews like the gunmen of New York whose crimes should not be charged up to the Jewish people. They said that was so but none the less I was to blame for using the expression. Finally just to show how completely fair-minded they were Felix handed me a scarcely veiled threat that the Jews would try to prevent my confirmation by the Senate. I didn't consider it worth while to take notice of it.[62]

Gibson described his discussion with Marshall in his diary:

M. clearly considered that it was his duty to conduct the case for the prosecution rather than endeavor to discover the facts and I had to do some pretty plain talking before we got down to brass tacks. I drew his statement to the papers on him and showed him clearly that each and every one of the twenty one statements he had made about me was the opposite of the truth. He wriggled and squirmed and reluctantly admitted that he had been wrong in each instance but did not give the slightest expression of regret or signify any intention of making amends for what I told him was a cowardly assault upon my character. I don't care a hang about the thing except so far as it is likely to interfere with my ability to carry out our plans for improving the conditions of the Jews. I hope I have given him a little light on the subject and that even if he doesn't do the decent thing he will refrain from messing things any more.[63]

Marshall, on the other hand, said after this meeting that the problem was „that whatever information Gibson received was solely from a single source and that his views were extremely one-sided".[64] Marshall stated that it was easier for Gibson "to converse with Polish officialdom that with those who have been the victims of that anti-Semitism which he recognizes but at the same time seeks in a sense to excuse". During their discussion Marshall also tried to convince Gibson "that it was the policy of the Jews to make friends with the Poles, and that it depended entirely upon the Poles as to whether or not they would take advantage of the industry and energy and the ability of their fellow-citizens".

Gibson also met in Paris with Lewis Strauss, one of the influential representatives of the American Jewish Committee. He wrote in his diary that at the end of two hours meeting he convinced Strauss that he was not "a Jew baiter" and that he really wanted to help "even if not in his simple way which consists chiefly in blackguarding the Polish Government for everything to be found in any report, no matter what is a source, its foundation or its inspiration".[65] Gibson also wrote in his diary about his discussions with other American Jewish leaders in Paris:

I find that most of these people are over wrought and have reached that stage where they unconsciously want to believe every exaggerated yarn about excesses against the Jews. They take it as prejudice if you question any story no matter whether they know where it comes from or not, so long as it makes out a case against the Poles and shows that the Jews are suffering. They are in a bad situation but you can't help the patient by treating him for an ailment he does not suffer from ... I can see that there will be a tremendous amount of patient talking to be done among the American Jews before they will be willing to abandon the idea of curing all the ills of their people by one blast at the Polish Government. They have got to make up their minds to work untiringly with the Government and not against it, and if they do I am convinced they can accomplish great things. If everybody can be got to tackle this thing from an ordinary common sense human point of view they can do one of the finest constructive tasks of modern times. If they can't I hate to think of the misery that will come.[66]

The meeting with Strauss, however, brought some improvement in the situation. The representatives of the American Jewish Committee went to the American Peace Mission in Paris and stated that the talks between Gibson and Strauss "were very satisfactory and that the atmosphere had been cleared".[67] At the same time Gibson once more told Felix Frankfurter and other Jews criticizing him that he did not intend "to let the mudslinging influence his desire to help the Jews in Poland" and that he would "hang himself" if the looked at the matter "through anybody's spectacles".[68] Gibson felt confident in this approach to the issue, since President Wilson and the State Department stood behind him. He wrote in his diary that they gave him "splendid support" and that he hoped to be able "to accomplish a great deal for the Jews of Poland even if it made harder by people who ought to be helping".[69]

On July 6 Gibson, in a confidential letter to Phillips, summarized his discussions with the American Jewish representatives in Paris, wondering what they really wanted to accomplish.[70] [Document No. 3] He wrote that they had made it clear to him that they did not care "to have any diagnosis made that is not made entirely on Jewish statements". According to Gibson, the propaganda campaign was conducted chiefly by American Jews without any regard for the welfare of the Jews in Poland; its purpose was "to weaken Poland in the interest of Germany which does not desire a formidable economic or political rival in the East". All of this was supposedly "a conscienceless and cold blooded plan to make the condition of the Jews in Poland so bad that they must turn to Zionism for relief".

Gibson's letter to Phillips accompanied a long report on the general situation of the Jews in Poland and on Polish-Jewish relations.[71] [Document No. 4] Gibson stressed that the Jewish question was one of the most complicated and delicate issues in Europe. It did not begin in the Polish territories with the signing of the armistice but had been introduced there earlier by the partitioning powers: "Jews with other minorities were subjected to hateful discriminations; public feeling was carefully aroused and maintained against the Jews as part of the system of dominating through internal dissention ... The Russian system was perhaps the worst". Gibson explained that he did not realize how this system worked until he came to Poland: "It was as cold blooded and fiendish as anything you can imagine and has reduced large classes of the Jews to a state approaching that of the animal". In a newly re-born Poland, legalized discrimination was gone but the prejudices and hatreds had survived; due to the absence of strong authorities, physical violence against the Jews spread all over the country, even to a greater degree than before. Gibson wrote that "several hundred Jews have been killed since last November but when one remembers that there are four millions of them in Poland, and when one bears in mind the upheavals through which the country has passed, and all the forces tending to create hatred of the Jews, this resolves itself into a mere symptom in the sickness of this part of the world". According to Gibson, the situation in Poland was "alarming" and required "immediate and earnest attention". What worried him was the state of public opinion, "more and more aggravated against the Jews".

Continuing his comments, Gibson stressed that the term "pogrom" should not be used to describe the outbreaks against the Jews in Poland, as the authorities did not support them and "did their best to preserve order". He divided anti-Jewish excesses into: 1) popular outbreaks, where prejudice against the Jews was released by the collapse of the Russian government and before the establishment of the Polish one; 2) events which occurred during fighting against the Bolsheviks, "under abnormal conditions and intense suspicion against the Jewish population", where Jews were killed either during street fights or were executed by the military; 3) spontaneous outbursts of anti-Jewish feelings arising from all sorts of causes and resulting in beating Jews, cutting their beards, looting their shops, etc. Gibson analyzed the events in Lida, Vilna, Pinsk, Lvov, Częstochowa, and Cracov in this context. He did not absolve the Poles of responsibility for killing Jews but, at the same time, described "the questionable" attitudes and behavior of some Jews, which were perceived by the local population to be anti-Polish. For Gibson, "the outstanding fact" was that religious discrimination did not exist; economic and social problems were the cause of conflicts. He also stressed that many incidents were instrigated by "American boys" from Haller's army.

Gibson believed that America could "render good service in helping to bring Poles and Jews together for discussion and constructive work but such service was delayed and hampered by the attempt of American Jews to hurt Poland in the eyes of the world". Such propaganda, Gibson felt, could be dangerous for Jews; if Poland were refused a foreign loan or certain frontiers, as a form of protest against her treatment of the Jews and other minorities, Poles could turn against them: "And if the people in their resentment do rise up and massacre Jews on a scale never before known, the blood guilt will be of the foreign Jews who with wicked disregard of the facts or the danger to human lives have played with this tremendously delicate situation".

Accenting his own influence on the Polish Government, Gibson stressed its good will and desire to stop the anti-Jewish outbreaks. According to him, the Government realized the gravity of the problem and wanted to find some solution to it. Unfortunately, the newly established authorities were not yet efficient enough to enforce their own orders. Moreover, the evidently anti-Semitic National Democrats, headed by Roman Dmowski, were very influential in Polish politics and public opinion, often disregarding the efforts of the Government. Nevertheless, Gibson believed that through education and patience the tensions between Poles and Jews might be overcome.

This lengthy report was much more thoughtful than the previous ones; it was not, however, made public by the State Department.

At that time, Gibson's argument about the lack of evidence to support Jewish charges of massive pogroms committed by Poles also received support from the American Embassy in Stockholm, which reported to Washington that the Soviet Government was using the Jewish issue in propaganda against the Poles.

The Soviet Government through the Bolshevik Telegram Bureau Rosta is at present sending out stories of alleged Jewish pogroms located in sections covered by the new advances of the armies of Kolczak, Denikin and the Poles. While anti-Jewish excesses might be expected to follow these victories as result of the very large Jewish participation in the Bolshevik movement, the Soviet Government appears to be using these in a special effort with this propaganda to win the support and sympathy of the world's Jewish population. For this reason reports of pogroms in these sections should be taken with reserve until the true facts are known.[72]

While the State Department generally supported Gibson's point of view, many Jews continued to criticize his reports. Louis Marshall summed up his opinion on this issue in a long letter he wrote to Abram Elkus, who earlier provided him with Gibson's dispatches and his correspondence with Phillips.[73] [*Document No. 5*] Marshall stated that most of Gibson's comments were „inaccurate and ill-digested", that Gibson gave the subject "merely superficial attention" and accepted the point of view "which makes the Jew the convenient scapegoat for all sins that have been inherited from the past and for all the misdeeds and incompetency of those in power". He rejected most of Gibson's findings. He said that Gibson was simply wrong in reporting that killings of Jews at Lvov, Vilna, Lida, Pinsk, Częstochowa and Cracov occurred during fighting against the Bolsheviks, when there were no Polish authorities yet established, or that they happened during spontaneous street fights or disputes about food prices.

Marshall argued that all these evens were "deliberate, continuous and unrelenting pogroms, atrocities and massacres". He accoused Gibson of abusing the term "justice", describing murders as "summary justice", terming humiliation of Jews by Haller's soldiers as only "minor persecution", or blaming the Jews for doing unfair business at the expense of starving Poland. He wrote Poles, not Jews controlled the food distribution in the country and that much of the economic discrimination against Jews was due to governmental policies. Marshall especially criticized Gibson for his remarks about American Jewry, whose propaganda supposedly hampered efforts to help Polish Jews and only "hurt Poland in the eyes of the world", and that for threatening American Jews "with responsibility for murders to be committed by the Poles because of their efforts to ameliorate the condition of their brethren". He said that the Jews in America knowing what was happening in Poland would always protest giving "publicity to these awful occurences, to ask for the intervention of the civilized Governments of the world to put an end to these monstrous brutalities" and that he "would personally rather die ten thousand deaths than to have been guilty of the crime of being silent". Marshall believed that all Polish Jews supported the Minorities Treaty and that Jews whom Gibson described as "assimilationists" were "few in number and either apostates or renegades, who were merely considering their private interests and their personal ambitions and who were justly detested by those whom they have not sought to help, though they were able to do so". At the end of his letter, Marshall stressed that Jews in America and England "appreciated fully the desirability of coming to an understanding with the Poles and of cultivating friendly relations with them", hoping that after ratification of the Minorities Treaty by the Polish Parliament, the persecution of Jews would cease.

2. THE MORGENTHAU MISSION

In May 1919, during the discussions in Paris about the protection of Jews in Eastern Europe, and after a series of Jewish protests in American cities, Herbert Hoover suggested that President Wilson send a special fact-finding mission to Poland to investigate Polish-Jewish relations.[1] The Polish Prime Minister, Ignacy Paderewski, who had strongly protested in Paris against the exaggeration of Polish offenses against the Jews, formally asked Wilson to send such a mission; he believed that it could make an objective report on the situation and thus help to improve Polish-Jewish relations. Gibson, for similar reasons, also supported the idea. With some delay, at the beginning of July, President Wilson accepted Hoover's and Paderewski's request and, after signing the Peace Treaties, appointed the members of the mission. They included Henry Morgenthau, former Ambassador to Turkey, an anti-Zionist and member of many Jewish philanthropic organizations; General Edgar Jadwin from the U.S. Corps of Engineers and Homer H. Johnson, professor of law at Case Western Reserve University in Cleveland.

Gibson was relieved to learn of the President's decision, thinking that now he would not be asked to make any more reports on Polish--Jewish relations. He wrote to the State Department that "it would seem futile for me to make further investigations".[2] Polk, however, thought that Gibson should complete the work he already had started. He cabled Lansing in Paris:

The Jewish leaders in this country appear satisfied to have Gibson, Bogen, and Bailey undertake this investigation and the Committee of Foreign Affairs is anxiously awaiting the completion of the Legation's report ... It seems to the Department important that the Legation complete the work which it has already begun. It has been publicly announced that the Legation was making this report. If, therefore, the Legation discontinues its investigation, the impression might be given that pogroms on a large scale actually had occurred, and that the Legation found it embarrassing to have further connection with the subject.[3]

Lansing did not share this view and supported Gibson's position. Answering Polk's cable he wrote:

Gibson has made a conscientious but necessarily brief inquiry into events at Vilna, Lida, Lvov and a number of other places. He finds, however, that the responsibility of these events is not always easy to place with entire justice; that the causes are often obscure and involve economic, social and political forces. He does not feel that he or anyone else can honestly undertake to give an opinion upon these events based upon such investigations as he can make while attending to other duties. He has therefore asked that a commission be appointed to devote its entire attention for as long a period as may be necessary to investigation of the relations between the Poles and Jews. This, of course, will involve a careful investigation of the various events complained of not only to establish the exact truth as to what has happened but to discover as accurately as may be the causes behind these events with a view to seeking a remedy for the situation, which he considers very bad and fraught with serious danger for the future. The President has appointed a commission composed of Mr. Henry Morgenthau, Mr. Homer Johnson and Brigadier General Jadwin who will proceed to Poland within a short time to study the whole question with a view to rendering constructive service to both the Polish State and the Jewish community. In as much as this commission is about to take up its duties Gibson feels that any fragmentary investigations that he could make would serve no useful purpose and the Mission holds the same view.[4]

Gibson in such a situation after returning to Warsaw from Paris conducted no further investigations of Polish-Jewish relations but continued to send reports on the issue to Washington. On July 4, he cabled about events in Warsaw on June 26, in which some soldiers from Haller's army chased and beat a number of Jews. "I am happy to report — Gibson wrote — that this riot which was not so serious as some others has stirred opinion here with beneficial results for whole Jew situation".[5] The Polish Minister of War issued a special order condemning the incident, warning the soldiers that "any violation of civil rights is a crime to be punished with full severity of law", and that they were "obliged while off duty or on duty to aid the oppressed".[6] He also made the officers responsible for the behavior of their soldiers. He suggested that inter-group tensions were caused "by the enemy agents paid to provoke them" which used "all sources and means of propaganda they possess intended to enfeeble the new state in process of formation". The War Minister told the soldiers, however, that disorderly behavior would "compromise them in the eye of Europeans and bring us the reproach of intolerance". Gibson wrote to the Department of State that "in view of this, as well as a similar pronouncement by the Minister of Interior and General Haller I submit that the Polish Government is at last acting with proper energy" and suggested that information about this "should be brought to the attention of interested persons in the United States".

Nevertheless, in some other cases the Polish authorities accused the Jews of directly causing outbreaks. For example,, Gibson transmitted to

Washington a *Note Verbale,* received from the Polish Ministry of Foreign Affairs, calling the attention of the American Legation at Warsaw to the fact that although such events "in the large majority of cases were by no means due to the anti-Semitic feelings on the side of the Christian population, but that they were generally results of the work of certain provokers".[7] The Ministry attached a judicial finding about one such event, in the town of Mszana Dolna, stating that this was "a new proof of the support of the fact that our army is daily exposed to provocations from certain elements of the Hebrew population".

On July 7, Gibson wrote to Leland Harrison of the American Commission to Negotiate Peace in Paris that many American Jews coming to Poland, especially the representatives of the Jewish Joint Distribution Committee, "abused the privileges accorded them to do anti-Polish propaganda in the country and gather material for scandalously untruthful articles which have been printed in the American press in connection with the present agitation".[8] Gibson wrote that there had been "one or two" American Jews "who had done us credit ... but as a rule these people seem to devote their efforts to knifing Poland". Gibson suggested that such Jews should be examined carefully before granting them passports to Poland.

At the same time Gibson had serious doubts to what extent the American Legation should be involved in Jewish affairs in Poland; if such involvement had to take place he wanted to have some Jews attached to it. He wrote to his friend Walter Lippman about this matter:

It seems to me to be far outside the boundaries of a diplomatic job. It is highly charged with bitterness and internal politics and no matter how well I handled it there would be serious danger of damaging the usefulness of the Legation. It had to be a Mission of some sort, and if its work is to be productive of much good I feel that there must be some Jewish representation on it.[9]

Gibson realized that outbreaks of group hostility were symptoms of serious problems. However, because this was the internal affair of a friendly state, the U.S. should investigate the issue only if she could come with concrete help to the people there. Gibson continued:

A good deal has happened here [i.e. in Poland] to the Jews since the signing of the Armistice, but the whole business is so wrapped up in doubt and misrepresentation and exaggeration that I don't think anybody will ever know just what happened in any one instance or just who was to blame and in what measure. Most of the worst trouble occurred in the fighting zone during actual hostilities when blood was hot and suspicion ran high. These things, to my mind, are not vitally important. They are only symptoms of what is far more important — a phase of the general sickness of this part of Europe which finds expression in anti-Jew feeling. I don't think it is any of our particular business as Americans to come here and investigate excesses if we intend to let it go at that. If we have any genuine and human interest in the welfare of the Jews I think we ought to find what happened, but merely as a step to finding out why it happened so that we can learn whether or not there is anything we can do to help the situation I am convinced there is a great deal we can do, but it will not be by making any reports on pogroms. It will be by much patient work and thought, endless forbearance with unreasonableness of all sorts. If we are prepared to tackle the question in this way we can go farther toward solving the pending problems than any other people I know of, and if we can accomplish anything substantial we shall have done a very big job and we can be proud of it. I don't look upon it as any picnic, and from some of the experiences I have had with this people we are trying to help, both in Poland and America, it has been made clear to me that it is not only a thankless job but one that is loaded with poison. However, I suppose in due time I shall get so I like poison and shall go ahead and do the best I can.[10]

Gibson also wrote in his diary:

I feel very strongly that American Jews can contribute materially to bettering the situation of the Jews in Poland ... The help [however] is certainly not coming through cursing the Polish Government. A great deal of the trouble is a heritage from the rotten old system of oppression and this can not be cured in a day. I am clamoring for a few level headed American Jews to come in here and w o r k and if they can be made to see that there is a great opportunity for service in plodding labor the end will be in sight. The Poles have got to work in the same way from their side and many of them are beginning to realize it.[11]

Meanwhile, Marshall's criticism of Gibson was widely reported by the Jewish press in Warsaw which demanded that Washington recall him from his post. The Polish press, for its part, strongly defended Gibson. The issue was also discussed in many newspapers in America.[12] The controversy was especially embarrassing, because of the imminent arrival of the Morgenthau Commission. Gibson, fully aware of the situation, cabled to the Department of State:

Marshall's statement ... in the *New York Times* has been printed here in Jewish press which has begun a vigorous campaign against me, demanding my recall on the authority of what Marshall says. Polish press has taken up the cudgels and question fills much space daily. Polish Government disposed to suppress one Jewish paper which was particularly offensive but I opposed this as not calculated to improve the situation. I am asking the Government unofficially to prevail upon Polish press to abandon campaign in my defense which only serves to keep feeling stirred up. Attacks on me in Jewish press of America based on Marshall's statement received here and serve Jewish press fresh ammunition. Personally I am not concerned over this campaign but it serves no useful purpose, particularly at a time when the President's Commission is about to begin its work. If, therefore, Mr. Marshall has made a subsequent statement of suitable character as was suggested by Messieurs. Elkus, Schiff, etcetera, it would be well to telegraph it here for publication.

The minorities treaty comes up before the Diet next week and [omission] needlessly although racial feeling is calculated to endanger its ratification. This is a good illustration of the danger of having American Jews without any accurate knowledge of the situation carry on an irresponsible propaganda in regard to such delicate matters.[13]

Gibson, in his diary, also described his reaction on the articles written about him in the Polish and Jewish newspapers:

The Polish papers are conducting a vigorous campaign on my behalf and the whole controversy getting more and more vicious each day. I today asked the F.O. [Foreign Office] to stop trying to defend me in the hope that the whole conflagration would die down for want of fuel. It is surprising that the Jews here turn and rend everybody who tries to help them unless he tackles the problem from the angle they dictate. It has discouraged a good many people to help them.[14]

As Marshall did not moderate his criticism of Gibson, Lansing cabled from Paris to the Department of State suggesting that it should issue a public statement about Gibson's investigations, emphasizing the fact that "agitation based on exaggerated reports can only aggravate the situation of the Jews".[15] Lansing, defending Gibson, proposed the following text of the statement:

Gibson accompanied by Bogen and Bailey has made visits to Vilna, Lida and Lemberg [Lvov] to investigate excesses against Jews. While he has acquired much information and a mass of statements valuable in defining the problem in its true proportions and showing the complexity of the facts to be considered, it is clear that unless he gives his entire time to this work over a long period he cannot hope to make a report on which final judgements can be based. The principal elements complained about seem to have occurred in the fighting zone either during a dual hostilities or immediately before the establishment of orderly government. The question of military necessity is important in each of these instances and this cannot be settled without exhaustive inquiry. Further, there are social, economic and other considerations which must be taken into account. As an instance of the intricacy of the questions involved it may be pointed out that Diet Commission investigating the Pinsk affair alone has been working steadily for over two months and has yet terminated its inquiry. Gibson soon reached the conclusion that he could not conscientiously undertake [omission] to base anything resembling a judicial finding on such incomplete investigation as he was able to make. His associates concur in this opinion. You will observe that the report on Vilna was chiefly confined to stating the conflicting assertions of the Poles and Jews and that neither Gibson nor his associates assumed [omission] to fix the measure of responsibility or blame. Accordingly several weeks ago Gibson recommended that some prominent American Jews or a commission with Jewish members be sent to Poland to go into the whole subject with a view not only to establishing the truth of the various reports but also to finding means ameliorating the situation of the Jews which he considers deplorable in many aspects. The President has appointed such a commission which will leave for Poland within a few days. Doctor Bogen has left for Paris and is not now available for further investigations. Any work of this sort undertaken by Gibson now would be merely duplication and would seem to serve no useful purpose.

Lansing also suggested that any public statement should stress "that Gibson whose reports have been characterized by fairness and desire to help the Jews will lend his full support to the Commission".

Bogen's name was mentioned in Lansing's cable because, at that time, Jewish newspapers in Poland and America learned that it was he who had co-signed the report about the Vilna affair (which denied that there had been a pogrom against the Jews), and they started a vigorous campaign against him. Bogen, accused of being "a Jewish traitor", had to abandon his relief mission in Poland.[16]

Some American Jewish leaders did not welcome the appointment of the Presidential Commission in general and questioned its composition in particular. They did not want to have any Jews in the group, especially not Morgenthau who did not sympathize with Zionist views.[17] Lippman was one of them. He wrote on this issue to Gibson:

I have no confidence whatever in Morgenthau. I don't think a Jew should have been on the commission, and I don't think there should have been any commision. I think the investigation should have been done by you and whatever help you needed attached to the Legation. I am sick to death of these travelling ignoramuses who stick their noses into a problem they don't understand and haven't time to investigate and who bring home the last bit of gossip someone stuffed into their ear.[18]

Morgenthau himself said that some Jewish leaders opposed him because they were "afraid of the truth" and only wanted to establish a case, not to determine the facts.[19] Therefore he had serious doubts about his participation in the Commission; eventually he was persuaded personally by President Wilson to accept the appointment.[20] Phillips described the situation in Paris in a letter to Gibson:

Elkus assured me that he, Schiff, and others are heartily in accord with you and your work and are diametrically opposed to the attitude of Louis Marshall as represented in his recent attacks upon the Legation. From the start I have taken Elkus into my confidence and have allowed him to read and to show other leading Jews here all of your despatches on "pogroms". I think this course has pleased them very much and that they were perfectly satisfied to have you handle the whole situation, as much so that they cabled to the President to delay the appointment of any other Commission of Inquiry. For your own information, they were strongly opposed to the appointment of Morgenthau on the Commission ... Realizing as I did the confidence which the [Foreign Relations] Committee had in you I was a little sorry myself to have the investigation taken out of your hands and placed in a Morgenthau Committee. On the other hand I appreciate that Morgenthau, being a Jew, might be in a position to get in touch with the Jews in Poland and talk to them like a "Dutch Uncle".[21]

In response to Wilson's decision, the American Jewish leaders in Paris decided to send Felix Frankfurter and Harold Gans to Poland as their own representatives, to carry on a separate investigation.[22] Gibson tried to stop their mission, knowing that Lansing too, was against the idea.[23] Gibson wrote to Harrison:

After seeing something of Frankfurter's general attitude on this question I feel that this would be deplorable and that he should not be given a passport. If he does come I shall be obliged to help him in his work or suffer the reproach of being anti-Jewish. If, on the other hand, I do the various things he will expect and he than goes out and makes a row about conditions in this country I shall be placed in an embarrassing position with the Polish Government and my influence will be weakened when next I want to be helpful to somebody who comes on a legitimate errand. The President has shown great interest in the welfare of the Jews in Poland. He has gone to the very unusual length of appointing a commission to come into this country and delve into its internal affairs. In these circumstances there is no earthly excuse for a private citizen to come in on the same errand, particularly as he has been outspokenly hostile to the President's commission and will come, if permitted, for a purpose of gathering material with which to combat the commission's findings.[24]

Gibson stressed in addition that the problem was not limited to the Frankfurter's case:

We are constantly refusing passports to non-Jewish Americans and seem to have no hesitancy in doing so ... I don't see any reason for a different policy toward American Jews who are out to make trouble and involve us in embarrassment with foreign Governments. I shall be glad to have some well balanced American Jews come in here on relief work of various sorts if they could keep out of propaganda and trouble making. But unfortunately nearly all those who have come have brought discredit on us by their performances here and after leaving the country ... It would be very helpful if you would have somebody go over the applicants for passports and cull out the names of pronounced Zionist nad other trouble makers. I feel very strongly that they should be kept out of this country at least until the commission has had an opportunity to do its work.

The Department of State, however, after consultation with Homer Johnson and Herbert Hoover, stated that "arrangements have gone too far to prevent Frankfurter from proceeding to Poland, and that it would not be advisable or expedient to stop him now even if it were possible".[25] Gibson continued to criticize Frankfurter after his arrival in Warsaw. He wrote to Harrison:

Just between us, I think the young man came here specifically for the purpose of making trouble and that he proposes to distort and misrepresent everything he has found. He is avowedly hostile to the man the Great White Father [President Wilson] picked out to handle the question and will get him if he can. I think the Great White Father's choice was 100 percent excellent. He [i.e. Morgenthau] is making a flying start, has injected a lot of horse sense into the situation and if he can be left alone for a little while I have high hopes that he will deliver a large supply of goods. If you can do anything to prevent others of the same sort from coming in here I think you will contribute considerably to the success of that particular job.[26]

Some tensions between Frankfurter, Gans and Gibson were inevitable but they did not expand to a full conflict. Gibson described the situation in a letter to Grew:

I did not in any way endeavor to prevent Gans and Frankfurter from carrying out the purpose of their mission. When they arrived I told them very plainly that the investigation of the Jewish question had been turned over entirely to Mr. Morgenthau and that I did not feel at liberty to go into the details of it with them or to present them to the Polish authorities. I told them that I would be glad to do anything in this regard that Mr. Morgenthau desired but that any independent action on my part in matters affecting the Jewish question now under investigation would be meddlesome. I was, however, entirely friendly and rather went out of my way to extend to Gans and Frankfurter the facilities of the Legation in forwarding their communications and I am forced to observe that they twice accepted my hospitality without any intimation that they considered me hostile to them. From their questioning of other people, however, I gather that they resented my unwillingness to lead them into Mr. Morgenthau's domain regardless of his desires. ... I understand that both Gans and Frankfurter expressed resentment that I should try to 'dissociate myself' from the

Jewish question during Mr. Morgenthau's visit. Frankfurter takes the ground that Mr. Morgenthau is totally unfitted for a position of this sort, which he elaborates in considerable and not very flattering detail, and that it is therefore my duty to hang onto the question. I am inclined to think that if the President of the United States has sufficient confidence in Mr. Morgenthau to entrust this question to him I can safely assume that he has enough sense to handle it without interference from me and that my job is to back him up to the hilt and help him in any way he thinks useful and that aside from this the matter is none of my business until Mr. Morgenthau and his Mission leave Poland, when I shall add that question to my many other sorrows.[27]

Gans, on the other hand, presented this matter in a different light, criticizing Gibson between the lines:

Even, if the tale ... had been true, and Frankfurter and I had to come here not only uninvited but in opposition to Mr. Morgenthau's wishes and for the purpose of checking up his activities with a view to subsequent criticism, we would have been within our clear and indubitable rights and any official who had expressed opposition to our coming or had sought to interfere with our attempt to secure such information as was open to the public, would have been guilty of a ridiculous exhibition of bureaucratic arrogance.[28]

The conflict between Frankfurter, Gans and Gibson did not develop further, however, and the Jewish representatives carried out their mission with no hindrance from the Legation.[29]

In the meantime, at the end of July and the beginning of August, the Jewish press in America printed a number of reports from Jews who had recently visited Poland, confirming information about the pogroms and discrediting Gibson's findings.[30]

Morgenthau's mission spent two months in Poland.[31] Its work was not free of controversy. On July 28, the Polish Telegraphic Agency cabled to the United States the text of an interview with Morgenthau, in which he supposedly stated that earlier information about pogroms was greatly exaggerated and that Polish Jews should lend greater support to the new Polish state.[32] The interview provoked a tempest in the Jewish community in America; the Jewish press accused Morgenthau of being a traitor to the Jewish cause. When he learned about this reaction, he denied having granted any such interview.[33] The Polish Telegraphic Agency, which realized that it was not in Poland's interest to antagonize Morgenthau and to put him in a difficult position, apologized for "a mistake" by one of its employees. The incident made Morgenthau realize once more how sensitive a job the mission had undertaken and how carefully American Jews were observing its work.

The Commission visited all the places where anti-Jewish excesses had taken place and talked with both Jewish and Polish representatives of different organizations, the local populace, witnesses to the outbreaks, and the victims.[34] The Commission was generally greeted very warmly.[35] Only a few Jews expressed doubts about the Commission, worrying that Morgenthau might share the common Polish belief in the danger of "Jewish Bolsheviks" and that he might think that the major issue was the fight against communism, which required a strong Poland not weakened by internal conflicts.[36] They questioned Morgenthau's appeals to the Jews in Poland's Eastern territories "to in no case assist the Bolshevist authorities" and "not to offer armed resistance against Polish troops" which would help "to avoid excesses and pogroms".[37]

The Commission's members and Gibson daily discussed all aspects of Polish-Jewish relations. Gibson wrote in his diary, that after seeing how Morgenthau evaluated the situation, he felt that the latter's judgment in the matter was "right" and that he "played the game well".[38] He wrote to Phillips:

I had already heard that some of our Jewish friends were opposed to Mr. Morgenthau's appointment. But I personally am very glad to have him. He made an excellent start and I am confident that if the report of the Mission is on the high plane that is now discussed by Mr. Morgenthau and his colleagues they will accomplish a great deal. As was probably inevitable he has ruffled the feathers of a good many people here and I shall feel better if he gets away without a real upheaval. It takes a certain amount of my time to do battle for him. My main effort is to convince people that if they will only be patient and let him finish his job without annoyance they will be well repaid for their forbearance, and I think we can hold the situation in hand here. I have no doubt that at the other end there will be some effort to undermine the Mission. I have heard some of the criticism that will probably be repeated at home and I hope you will take it with a large grain of salt and give the Mission time to produce results in its report.[39]

On August 12, Morgenthau wrote a letter to Herbert Hoover, who was visiting Poland at that time, sharing with him his views on Polish--Jewish relations.[40] He stated that everybody admitted that in this country "a strong prejudice against the Jews prevailed", but "animosity of the Poles towards the Jews has been greatly aggravated by the success of the Jewish committee in Paris in ... compelling the Poles to grant to the Jews the rights conceded under the separate treaty with Poland" which "deeply wounded" Polish pride. Morgenthau, describing the situation in Poland, wrote that the Poles were "almost in a state of despair at the fearful task that confronts them to solve their problems ... as they are without food, fuel, raw material, transportation, trained government officials, a constitution, and practically every other necessary thing to bring to their people any direct benefits from this great freedom which circumstances, as much as their own efforts, have thrusted upon them". After investigating Polish-Jewish relations for a month already, Morgenthau realized the difficulty of his task:

A white-washing report, or even a softened statement of the mishaps, will not satisfy the aroused American and English opinion. Any report that comes short of the truth will be completely shattered by the publication of the detailed facts which are in the possession of the Jewish leaders of America and England. It requires absolute honesty, and a grim determination to face the truth and remedy it, and not shifting of responsibility or blame, or a mere dodging of the issues. And unless this is done, Poland will start her new life with more toxin in her system than she can possibly absorb.

Morgenthau then went so far as to propose that Hoover appoint another commission of experts in various fields, who would be "willing to live in Poland for at least one year and make a complete survey of the conditions of the country, employ an adequate force of assistants, and work out the solution for the entire Jewish question". He was even ready to donate the then large sum of 25,000 dollars to cover the expenses of such a mission. Finally, Morgenthau called on Hoover to demonstrate the interest of American Christians in this matter by attending some large meeting in a Jewish synagogue in Warsaw.[41]

After spending two months in Poland, the Commission returned to Paris and its members started to work on the final report. Gibson had been in Paris for a few days when Morgenthau arrived from Poland and met him there. He wrote in his diary:

I had lunch with Mr. Morgenthau and heard his views of all sorts of things, including an outline of his report which will be satisfactory if he can get through the actual writing. He writes with great difficulty and has to have an impresario to whip his ideas into shape. He wanted me to stay on here and help him grind out his report but as I am an interested party I am trying to have as little to do with it as possible. All the time the Mission was in Poland I studiously stayed away from their meetings and hearings and I don't propose to slip into it now, though I would do a lot to help the old gentleman in anything else.[42]

The members of the Mission could not agree on the conclusions. As Gibson was already back in Warsaw, Morgenthau wrote him:

We had no end of arguments in trying to agree in a joint report — we finally concluded to hand in separate reports. The authorities at the White House are displeased I have smothered both reports. This may prove the advisable course.[43]

Jadwin and Johnson discussed this matter in their introduction to the report and presented in it "the official" explanation:

After the return of the mission to Paris its members were unable to consult together on account of the absence of Gen. Jadwin on other duty in southern Russia. Mr. Morgenthau before leaving Paris submitted a report representing his views of the situation, and the other members, in his absence, have prepared these considerations, which, while differing but slightly from Mr. Morgenthau's, have been put in the form of a complete report as leading up to conclusions which differ from those of Mr. Morgenthau.[44]

Jadwin and Johnson wanted Gibson to come to Paris again to examine their report before they presented it to the President. Gibson asked Grew for his opinion and was advised not to do so, "to be able to prove an alibi in the future".[45] The problem lasted for a while and even later, in New York, Phillips tried to get members of the Commission together and agree on one version but was unsuccessful.[46]

In the Fall both the Morgenthau and Jadwin and Johnson reports were submitted to President Wilson. They described in detail the situation in Poland and Polish-Jewish relations. Morgenthau stressed that out of eight major excesses which occurred in 1919 (neither report used the term "pogroms" as inadequate to the character of the events), only two took place in the ethnically Polish territories, four involved poorly disciplined soldiers in combat zones, and one was the result of a junior officer's orders. In most cases, the outbreaks were investigated by authorities, and those found guilty were sentenced. Morgenthau wrote:

Just as the Jews would resent being condemned as a race for the action of a few of their undesirable coreligionists, so it would be correspondingly unfair to condemn the Polish nation as a whole for the violence committed by uncontrolled troops or local mobs. These excesses were apparently not premeditated, for if they had been part of a preconceived plan, the number of victims would have run into the thousands instead of amounting to about 280. It is believed that these excesses were the result of a widespread anti-Semitic prejudice aggravated by the belief that the Jewish inhabitants were politically hostile to the Polish State.[47]

Morgenthau, commenting on the investigation in his diaries, wrote that there was "no question that some of the Jewish leaders exaggerated these evils".[48] He also criticized "malevolent, self seeking mischief makers both in the Jewish and Polish press and among the politicians of every stripe" and the Zionists in general.[49]

The Jadwin and Johnson report was much more comprehensive; it presented the complex causes of the outbreaks and suggested a variety of concrete steps to the Polish authorities and the outside world to help the country and its minorities.[50] The authors stressed both the German and Russian efforts to incite Poles against the Jews and the foreign anti--Polish propaganda from which the country seriously suffered. They directed their readers' atention to the fact that, while Poland "has always shown complete religious tolerance, and equal rights for all citizens has always been the permanent postulate of all the parties ... some representatives of the Jewish national movement ... refused to subordinate the Jewish question to the general needs of the Polish State". They believed that none of the reported excesses "were instigated or approved by any governmental authority, civil or military", while anti--Semitic attitudes had their roots "in the history and the attitude of the Jews, complicated by abnormal conditions produced by the war". Jadwin and Johnson wrote that they "were assured by many representative Jewish delegations that while they were disturbed by the anti-Jewish feelings ... they did not fear for their lives or liberty". They believed that, since Poland accepted the Minorities Treaty, Polish-Jewish relations would improve.

Finally, on January 15, 1920, the Morgenthau and the Jadwin-Johnson reports were sent by President Wilson to the Senate and were published in the Congressional Records.[51] As the reports basically did not confirm the information about pogroms in Poland, the House Committee on Foreign Affairs stopped further investigation of the issue.

The Polish American community greeted the reports rather favorably, especially the one written by Johnson and Jadwin, which was more positive about the Poles. The Jewish press ignored them almost completely.[52] The *Dearborn Independent,* an anti-Semitic newspaper, even suggested that Jews were blocking their distribution.[53] Morgenthau himself was strongly criticized by the Zionist for pro-Polish attitudes. On the other hand, the Polish Minister to Washington, in his report to Warsaw, accused him of taking a very critical stand toward Poland in speeches delivered to Jewish audiences in number of American cities in which he tried "to rehabilitate himself".[54] Gibson wrote to Phillips:

I have seen little repercussions in the press from time to time about the struggles of the Morgenthau Mission to agree upon a report, and imagine you must have had a rather strenuous time. Mr. Morgenthau apparently could not resist the temptation to show his report to some people at least for I have had comment on it and I notice that he made at least one speech in which he gave a very curious account of the trouble at Pinsk. I am sorry that his courage did not carry him far enough to say in public what he was ready enough to say in private.[55]

Despite these controversies, Gibson was satisfied. The Commission's reports, both in terms of the description of the course of outbreaks and in conclusions, were close to his earlier findings and opinions. In general, however, these reports did not contribute much to mitigating tensions between Polish and Jewish communities, neither in Poland, nor in the United States.

3. THE CONTINUING PROBLEM

The Morgenthau commission reports did not end the controversy over the situation of the Jews in Poland and Polish attitudes toward them. In the Fall of 1919, American Jews representing different organizations continue to arrive in Poland to investigate the matter. Gibson believed that many of them abused their status in the country and embarked upon a prejudiced campaign against Poles and the Polish government. On October 15 he wrote a confidential letter to his friend Leland Harrison about this issue again.

Practically ever since I have been here we have had a steady stream of American Jews either in official positions or with official backing and recommendation coming in here to gather material for anti-Polish intrigue. Most of them have come ostensibly for purely relief work, which we in the Belgium Relief always considered entailed a moral obligation not to concern ourselves with anything but relief work. One came in the uniform of the Y.M.C.A., and a number have brought letters of introduction from people high in authority. There is hardly an instance of an American Jew coming into Poland on relief work or any of the various "missions" they have assumed who has not, after leaving the country, come out with attacks upon Poland...[1]

After citing examples of such Jews, Gibson continued:

The record of American Jews abusing their passports and the privileges accorded them here is both shameful and embarrassing to us, and I think the time has come when positive action should be taken by our Government. It is certainly preferable to stop this sort of thing of our own motion before the patience of the Polish Government is exhausted and they point out to us the unfriendliness of our action in permitting our people with official support to carry on a concerted effort to undermine this country and its Government. We in the United States would not for a moment tolerate intrigue against the Federal Government or the people of the United States by any series of Poles who might come over to exploit the treatment of the Negroes or the Japanese. We would give them short shrift and it is only the unbelievable patience of the Polish Government that has saved us from having several very unpleasant incidents here. I don't know what the present status of the passport restrictions is, but if we still have any say about who can and who cannot come to Poland we ought, from motives of decency and self-protection, to look these people over very carefully before they are allowed to have a visa for Poland ... Why don't you turn this matter over in your mind and in the light of your knowledge of the present passport situation take the matter up with the Department. I should like to have some definite steps taken by us before we have a public scandal.

Harrison answered Gibson that the Department of State could not do much about it:

As you know it is very difficult, if not impossible, for the Department really to control the movements of such persons or to refuse them passports or visas when they have backing in certain quarters. My own feeling is that from now on it is entrirely up to the Poles to keep undesirable foreigners out of Poland. But please don't think me unsympathetic, and be sure that I will do everything I can to help you out.[2]

In the Fall of 1919 and in the Spring and Summer of 1920, killings among local populations in the Eastern territories during the Polish--Soviet war gave the Jewish press in America a new reason to blame the Poles for organizing pogroms and persecuting the Jews.[3] As many Jews were among the victims, serious questions arose on many occasions as to whether the casualties were caused by military actions or by the anti-Semitism of the population. Some newspapers again expressed doubts about the rectitude of granting "immature Poles" independence (recognizing it as Wilson's mistake) and supported the Soviet offensive, believing that the situation of the Jews in these territories would improve under the Russian government.[4] Gibson held quite contrary views. On February 14, 1920, he wrote to the Secretary of State a new and long report on this issue.[5] [Document No. 6] According to him, the 1919 anti-Polish agitation was "characterized by gross exaggeration ... and although it had a momentary success it was eventually discredited when the truth became known". This was why, at that moment, American Jews, according to Gibson, were considering either developing a new campaign about massacres of the Jews in the Ukraine "with a consistent endeavor to confuse that country and Poland so far as possible" or withdrawing all Jewish relief workers "with a statement that they were driven out by Polish persecution".

Gibson was convinced that the group which carried on the anti-Polish agitation was not representative of the whole of American Jewry, but he was worried that the majority of American Jews was "merely misled" by them. Gibson wrote that "they stand to do much more harm that good and if in their ignorance the present campaign of international intrigue continues to receive their misguided support, we must frankly anticipate the growth of anti-Jewish feeling in the United States". Next, Gibson stressed that the Jews in Poland never took any significant part in the anti-Polish agitations and themselves criticized the approach taken by American Jewry, which had not consulted Polish Jewry and was inspired "chiefly by selfish motives of promoting their own ends".

Gibson argued that foreign agitation created much resentment among the Poles and that more intelligent Jews were afraid of serious consequences from it in the future. After talking to many American Jews who had come to Poland, he said he was unable "to discover anything beyond a desire either for agitation for its own sake, to punish Poland as a whole for what has happened to the Jews, or ... to make her economic and political situation as difficult as possible ... as if Poland were to be sufficiently intimidated through propaganda, she would submit to any conditions imposed upon her in the inteerst of the Jews". Describing the situation in Poland, he expressed his opinion that the so-called Jewish question was entirely social and economic, not religious, and that economic discrimination against the Jews was made easier by their separateness and distinctiveness. He believed that the only way to make the life of Jews "less intolerable" was to improve the general economic condition of the country. Anti-Polish agitation, weakening Poland politically and economically, would then have only a disastrous effect on Jews. This was why Gibson believed that American Jews should "silence the people who were inspired only by blind hatred and a desire to intrigue" and should "suppress improper activity and work constructively". Gibson also suggested a radical change in the personnel of the Jewish relief organizations in Poland, leaving only native American citizens, because those who were born in Poland in Russia "maintained prejudices and hatreds of their native countries". At the end of his report, Gibson expressed his worry that, if that did not happen, "we must be prepared for conflicts, intrigues, and agitation which would be harmful to our country and to Poland and which would react unfavorably on the situation of the Jews here".

The Department of State, however, did not want to become involved again in any dispute with American Jewry and did not respond to Gibson's propositions.

In the Summer of 1920 Gibson, on home leave, received an unexpected request from Louis Marshall, one of the founders of the Joint Distribution Committee, to address a large Jewish gathering of this organization in New York City.[6] [Document No. 7] During the ceremonial dinner, Gibson was praised highly for his relief efforts. He described the event in a letter to his mother:

It would have amused you to hear the praises of your son from the same men who were trying with all their strength to skin him alive last year. The same Louis Marshall who was denouncing me in the New York papers made a speech which was fit to be engraved upon my tombstone — that is if I had a few acres of tombstone. The others followed in the same strain and before I got through I had a high opinion of myself. Anyway it got them on record.[7]

Marshall probably did not really change his critical opinion of Gibson but decided to praise him at that moment for his own political reasons.

In the late Fall of 1920, American Jewish leaders started to limit their criticisms of Poland. On November 10, 1920, a special conference of American Jewry formulated its official standpoint toward Poland and handed it to a Polish Minister in Washington, Count Kazimierz Lubomirski in the form of a memorandum. This resolution, signed among others by Louis Marshall, in the name of the American Jewish Committee, and by Stephen Wise, in the name of the American Jewish Congress stated:

So far as Poland is concerned we desire to place upon record that the Jews of the United States are not now and never been hostile to that land. On the contrary, they have at all times sympathized with the aspiration of the Polish people for the restoration of their freedom. Because of that fact and because of our anxiety to promote the welfare of the millions of our brethren who now live and will continue to live in Poland, whose ancestors have for centuries lived there and regarded it as their home, we are deeply interested in the perpetuation of the present free and independent Republic of Poland ... In giving utterance to these sentiments we would, however, be lacking in candor if we failed to voice our grave concern at the treatment to which our brethren have been subjected in Poland for some time past ... While the Jews of America stand ready and willing to aid in the creation of a prosperous Poland, they feel justified in entertaining the expectation that Poland shall remove all obstacles that stand in the way of cooperation by the Jews of Poland in the attainment of what should be the united purpose of all the inhabitants of Poland — its social, economic, civic and political development.[8]

In Poland, in March, 1921, a constitution was adopted by the Parliament, which guaranteed all rights for Jews and other minorities. Marshal Józef Piłsudski was in power and tensions between Poles and Jews seemed to calm down for a while. Gibson did not report on Polish-Jewish affairs for quite some time. It was only in January, 1922, that he wrote on this subject again discussing the situation in Vilna during the Polish-Lithuanian military dispute over that city and the surroundings. He described a plan for a government, proposed by some Jewish leaders in this multi-national community.

The Jews are strongly nationalist in sentiment and are demanding not the guarantees of a minority treaty such as were secured for them in Poland but equal rights within the state on a confederate basis. This plan was outlined in great detail by Rabbi Rubenstein, leader of the Jewish Party in Vilna. The theory is that each of the four nationalities in the Vilna and Kowno districts should be represented in the central Government by a minister who would be empowered to protect their rights. Each nationality should have separate schools supported by collectors responsible to the Minister in the central Government. Each nationality should have its own court for general jurisdiction on which each nationality has proportional representation, the question of foreign policy to be decided by the Council of Ministers. Something approximating this plan has been tried in the Kowno-Lithuanian State, where great advances had been made to the Jews in a shrewd play on the traditional antagonism of the Poles towards the Jews in the hope of securing the sympathy and support of the large Jewish population.[9]

This kind of solution was strongly criticized by the Poles, who again accused the Jews of anti-Polish behavior in an attempt to create "a state within a state". Gibson shared the Polish view.

Gibson was fully aware of the fact that one of the reasons for the Polish-Jewish conflict, especially in the Eastern territories, was the common perception the Poles had of strong Jewish involvement in the Communist movement. He presented his thought on this issue to the Secretary of State in February, 1922:

One of the more popular theories about Bolshevism is that it is an almost exclusively Jewish movement and one of the steps in the "Great Jewish World Conspiracy". There is no doubt that the individuals in control of the Soviet machinery are Jews in an overwhelming proportion but I have never seen anything to prove the existence of a Jewish world conspiracy, or to show that Bolshevism is a Jewish movement. However, it does seem clear the reasons for Jewish predominance among the leaders of Bolshevism are perfectly natural. It must be remembered that during many generations the Jews in the old Russian empire were subjected to frightful persecution and oppression of a sort calculated to turn their active minds toward subversive doctrines. Despite all this oppression they clung tenaciously to education, and amid the great mass of ignorant Russians they alone were able to read and to discuss with intelligence the revolutionary literature so widely disseminated in tracts and pamphlets. The ignorance of the Russian peasant protected him against these seditious influences, while the education and intelligence of the Jews exposed them to it. As a result, when this Bolshevist movement broke out and an opportunity was offered for putting these doctrines into practice, the people equipped for the work were largely Jews. In matters of political doctrine they have not been largely of one mind at all and have been divided by petty disagreements. It has been inevitable that individual Jews have grown steadily in power under the Soviet system, and that the superficial impression should have been generally thought that Bolshevism was a Jewish movement.[10]

In November, 1922, Gibson once again wrote to Washington about anti-Polish agitation allegedly carried on by some American Jews.[11] [Document No. 8] In a strictly confidential dispatch, Gibson described how he had been approached by a number of Jews "with alarming stories of what has happened and what is going to happen". They complained to him about what they called "pogroms", which were, in fact, "food disorders", during which both Jewish and Christian merchants were injured. Gibson questioned the purpose of the American Jewish Committee's gathering and publishing all possible reports that referred to the mistreatment of Jews. According to him, Jewish leaders accepted for the purpose of agitation any allegations made by a Jew against the Poles, any newspaper report or anonymous statement, so long as it indicated that a Jew had been unfairly treated.

Gibson then recalled Marshall's "scurrilous attack" on him back in 1919 and his "completely false statements" as to what Gibson had said in confidential reports "which he had not seen and which he did not even ask to see before assuming the responsibility for making a newspaper attack". Gibson wrote that, for Marshall, such behavior was completely justified simply by the fact that his reports "were causing great harm to Jewish propaganda", while the issue itself was not important. Gibson also suggested that although Marshall "was obliged to admit the falsity of his statements in the presence of several witnesses, he did not consider it necessary to make any amends, and has allowed his misstatements to stand to this day". Next, Gibson presented his opinion about the politics of American Jewry with regard to the problems of the Jews in Poland and the actions the American Government should, or should not, undertake in this matter. He stated that some Jewish leaders in Poland used the threat of American intervention as a political weapon to support their demands during the Parliamentary debates.

Gibson criticized this approach. He was convinced that any American intervention on behalf of the Polish Jews could do them "nothing but harm" and, at the same time, could damage the United States' interests. He wrote that the organized Jews in Poland were "deliberately and openly anti-Polish", that the Jewish press constantly "hurls abuse at the Polish Government and people and calls down upon them every imaginable curse", and that "the daily run of Jewish callers at the Legation and Consulate General are loud in their denunciations of Poland, its Government and people, and frequently express annoyance if their sentiments do not elicit approval from American representatives". Gibson stated that despite all the agitation by American Jewish organizations about alleged pogroms in Poland, it was established by Morgenthau's Commission that the number of Jews killed there in 1919 "was less than the number of Negroes killed in the United States during the same period". Moreover, all of them happened immediately after the collapse of the three empires which occupied Poland, "when all the restraints were withdrawn and all hatreds and prejudiced were unleashed", while Blacks were killed in America during times of peace, with none of the excuses to be found in Poland.

According to Gibson, Jews in Poland demanded not equal but exceptional treatment: exemption from military service and from certain taxes, separate courts with Jewish laws, separate Jewish schools at the government's expense, etc. Gibson wrote that in order to obtain these demands they resorted to any tactics that would place the Poles in an unfavorable position. They not only did not cooperate in building a Polish State but endeavored to frustrate the settlement of Polish problems "by interference, threats and non-participation". Gibson believed that, when the Jews pressed their demands and for the intervention of the United States, they did it "not to prevent cruelties and injustices to an oppressed minority but to secure the aid of a large power for their selfish ends in a matter which is a purely internal problem of a friendly state".

Gibson also believed that even a mild American intervention into

Jewish matters in Poland would establish a precedent which could enable Jewish leaders to bring pressure to bear upon the American Government and the Congress to undertake similar actions in Soviet Russia, "which might well jeopardize our national interests without any compensating advantage to the Jews". According to Gibson, as "there is a strong conviction in the minds of the common people here and in Russia that the Soviet regime is in the hands of the Jews, and that their oppression is Jewish oppression", any change in this country can bring "a massacre of Jews on a scale unprecedented in modern times".

Washington once more did not react to Gibson's note. The Department of State did not want to be involved in Polish-Jewish relations. In the following years the entirety of American foreign policy became more isolationist again, and Polish affairs were not high on its agenda. Even when leaders of American Jewry directly demanded that the American Government take some action against what they perceived as further persecution of the Jews in Poland, the Department of State answered that no intervention was formally possible or necessary since it concerned matters which did not "directly affect American citizens or interests".[12]

* * *

How should Hugh Gibson's views of the Jewish issue in Poland and of Polish-Jewish relations be evaluated? It is not possible to answer this question without looking at it in the broader context of his performance in Poland and of Jewish politics at the time. Gibson was a skilled and devoted diplomat trying to serve his country in the best possible way. Fully supporting the idea of the responsibility of the great powers for world peace and for the future of the new states emerging after World War I, he became deeply involved in Polish affairs (although he often thought that the U.S. was crossing the bounds of interference in the purely internal affairs of a foreign country). Gibson would have like Poland to play the role of a balance between Germany and Russia and of a solid buffer protecting the West from Communism. But Poland in 1919 could play no such role. The country was ruined after years of occupation and the war, and it badly needed unification of its distinct parts, establishment of authority and borders, overcoming of famine and typhus, and a solution to the conflicts existing with its neighbors nations and its own minorities. In the endless list of priorities for this re-born state, Gibson, like the Poles, did not place the improvement of the situation of Jews at the very top. He was much involved in relief efforts for the whole population, not for Jews in particular. He was also not fearful of the future of Polish-Jewish relations, as he believed that the antagonism between the two communities was a legacy of the politics of the partitioning powers, Russia in particular, which would diminish when the country achieved a stage of normalcy. He trusted that the new Polish Government would fully respect the rights of the Jews and other minorities. In this context, he perceived campaigns of protest by some Jewish groups abroad as unnecessary, undertaken without understanding the situation in Poland and without the support of the most interested party — the Polish Jews. Gibson believed that this kind of behavior was turning the attention of world leaders and the public from the more important tasks of the moment and was weakening the position of Poland on the international scene.

Gibson, working in very difficult conditions in the newly established Legation in Warsaw, during dramatic moments in postwar Poland, tried to present the full picture of the Polish situation to Washington. Despite his intentions, however, his reports were not always accurate. This criticism applies also to his approach to Jewish issues. While some reports coming from people who visited Poland at the time were often one-sided, and less than objective in presenting Poland's problems, in particular, exaggerating the extent of pogroms against the Jews, Gibson's writings, in turn, sometimes wrongly described the behavior of Jews toward Poles and lacked understanding of the scale of the anti-Semitism existing in these territories and of its possible consequences. Thus, during the Paris Peace Conference Gibson was led into a clash with a part of American Jewry for whom his way of presenting the situation in Poland became an obstacle to achieving international guarantees protecting the Jews in Eastern Europe from pogroms and mistreatment. Analyzing different Gibson's statements and actions it is difficult, however, to fully accept the thesis of his anti-Semitism. It was rather his lack of full understanding of certain problems which causes his conflicts with some American Jews. It is no doubt, however, that in the history of Polish-Jewish relations after World War I this first American Ambassador to Poland played an important and not to be forgotten role.

DOCUMENTS

Document No. 1

Cable, Gibson to the Acting Secretary of State [Frank Polk]

Warsaw, June 2, 1919.

114. For Mision and Department. I venture to submit the following observations which it is desirable to bear in mind in connection with the questions affecting the Jews in Poland.

1. The Jews should not for all purposes be considered as a whole. There are very clearly separate[d] classes and the distinctions are generally recognized by the Poles. These may be indicated as follows:

(a) The assimilators. The element of patriotic and respected Jews who are assimilated to the body of Polish citizens and are not involved in the so called Jewish question. They occupy Government positions and have no grievances against the Polish state. They look upon their religion purely as a religion and not as a nationality.

(b) The orthodox Jews. Chiefly engaged in trade and manufacture, peddling, et cetera. Although not aggressive they are as a rule indifferent to Polish state. Among them is an educated element, professional men, et cetera, who profess loyalty to Poland.

(c) The Litwaks. Russian Jews whose coming to Poland was attributable to two causes: (1) The planting of spies, agents, provocateurs, et cetera, as a part of the old Russia[n] system. (2) A far greater number simply deported to get them out of Russia proper. These people are avowedly hostile to the Polish Government and give open provocation to public feeling. They are as a rule better educated than the run of the Jews in Poland and like type are wealthy.

(d) The criminal class. A troublesome class composed chiefly of young Jews who have abandoned the tenets of their religion and live largely by their wits, a class that is not unlike the gun men in New York and give constant trouble to the police.

2. The Jewish question in Poland is not in any sense religious but social and economic. Neither Poles nor Jews refer to religious differences in discussing the question [of] social problems.

(a) A large element of Jews persist in looking upon their religion as a nationality. Their attitude toward the Poles [in this respect] is often hostile and provocative. The attitude of the Jewish press and Jewish members of the Diet serve to intensify ill feeling. These believe that they can coerce Poland through the influence of foreign Jews upon their Governments. This situation is not helped by the attitude of Polish newspapers [many of] which keep feeling stirred up on constant discussion of Polish grievances against the Jews.

(b) Under the old oppressive rulers it was known that spies and agents provocateurs for Russia, Germany and Austria, were continually recruited from the Jewish ranks. More recently bandits and spies for the Bolsheviki, the Ukrainians and Germans have been recruited in the same way. This does not mean that the Jews as a class have done these things but it is an undoubted fact that many of the agents who have been apprehended have been Jews who have sought to impair military operations in the war zone, cutting telephone and telegraph wires. Their behavior towards the troops has rought about what is at present the worst phase of the problem. The soldiers are generally convinced that Jews are carrying intelligence to the enemy, firing on them from houses et cetera. The result is a dangerous state of feeling. It is to be noted that all the important incidents in which Jews have recently been killed were troubles (in?) Lemberg [Lvov], Pinsk, and Chenstokhov [Częstochowa]. Great difficulty is now being experienced by the commanders of Haller's troops [1] in controlling anti-Jewish action. The Polish officers with these troops are men who have come from Russia since the Bolshevik regime [and] who have seen the Jew as a Bolshevik or his agent in nefarious practices. The soldier who comes from America is first amused by the Jewish costume, beard and habits and then incensed by the Jew's lack of patriotism and his speech. In view of the misery on every side, his sense of justice is easily aroused.

Economic problems. In former times there was no Polish class to occupy the middle ground between peasant and noble landowners. The Jews came in and occupied that place without resistance. As time went on a Polish middle and merchant class grew up and that matter was in a fair way to adjustment when in 1905 Russia drove many of her Jews across the border into Poland. This reestablished the preponderance in trade of the Jews and intensified the feeling. In parts of the country the Jews have a practical monopoly of trade particularly in food stuffs and consider that this has made one of the most dangerous phases of the question. There is no doubt that this class carries on business by methods that would not be tolerated in the United States but that has been permitted under the old form of tyranny and cannot be quickly corrected by Governmental action. Now they hoard food to keep prices up and indulge in profiteering. How far Christians have gone in for these detestable practices I have not been able to determine but the fact is that most of the food shops belong to Jews and the resentment for these practices falls upon them. The situation is aggravated by the fact that there is in Poland a large population of unemployed largely of the turbulent sort to be found in mining and manufacturing communities. When they see food which they cannot buy because of high prices they resort to violence. Another grievance is that Jews smuggle food through the military lines into Germany and into territory occupied by the Germans. This is an organized business and smugglers licenses are issued by the German authorities permitting these people to pass freely for the recognized purpose of smuggling food out of Poland. Incidents that occur in this connection have no religious tinge. If a Jew is injured it is called a pogrom. If a Christian is mobbed it is called a food riot.

3. The present campaign abroad is largely based on agitation fomented outside of Poland. The Jews here complain of their treatment in general and refer on all occasions to the Pinsk affair in regard to which I have reported fully, and for the past day or two to Czenstokhov [Częstochowa]. They make no reference to general hardships [massacres] such as are reported in the foreign press and I judge that they consider these two affairs their principal grievances. I learn from Lieutenant Colonel Dawley General Staff that there is a German news agency established at Kovno which is in German hands and that this agency is pouring out [to Berlin] a stream of stories as to what is happening in the [neighboring] regions under Polish occupation. These articles are copied in the press of Scandinavia and other countries whence comes [a great] part of the present agitation. The Germans are clearly doing this with a purpose: (a) to stir up as much dissension as possible inside the country so as to keep it in a weakened condition and (b) to create the impression throughout the world that Poland is a country unworthy of our support or sympathy, thereby weakening her as a possible rival or enemy. This German propaganda is certainly not undertaken for the altruistic purpose of helping the Jews.

4. Our aim in this mater, I take it, is to exert any proper effort to prevent violence or discrimination against the Jews and to contribute so far as may be to a better understanding between the races.

5. Solution is only possible through the elimination of the present distrust and dislike which is largely artificial and in order to accomplish this I see the following possibilities:

(a) To prevail upon the local press both Polish and Jewish to moderate its tone. I have had some talks on the subject and believe that a certain amount can be accomplished in this direction.

(b) To call upon the assimilator Jew to throw off his present passive attitude and take an organized active part in assisting the Polish Government to solve this problem both through advice and example as well as actual efforts with their own coreligionists. American Jews can play an important part in starting such a campaign.

(c) I believe there is a good deal of misapprehension as to the attitude of the United States on the question both among Poles and Jews to the effect that we are advocates of the Jews as such as against the Poles. This is used as a lever by the Jews and is a cause of resentment and distrust among the Poles. This might be helped providing some representative Poles could visit England and the United States to study the Jewish question along constructive lines.

(d) Violent agitation abroad based on unwarranted reports of conditions cannot help the Jews has exactly the opposite effect. Such propaganda when it becomes generally known here, will rightly or wrongly be attributed in some measure to the Jews and resentment will be intensified. After such agitation has been discredited, it will be difficult to secure credence for real grievances when they arise. I believe that the Department can render a service to the Jews of Poland by discouraging agitation based upon exaggerated or unfounded reports.

(e) The Department can contribute to the solution of this problem by: (1) facilitating the coming [to] Poland of American Jews who are prepared to face facts honestly and work patiently for the good of their coreligionists; (2) refusing passports to agitators of any sort, Jewish or Christian. We have had unfortunate experiences with both kinds.

6. A great problem which is the product of time and circumstances requires both patience and good will for its solution. Solution is deferred by agitation which is productive of ill will on both sides. The Government is [well intentioned] but lacks power and experience in authority. It is amenable to suggestion to an extent that is surprising. I should be glad therefore to receive ideas from the Department or from anybody sincerely interested in the problem.

Gibson

Source: FR, pp. 757—760.

Document No. 2

Cable, Gibson to the Acting Secretary of State [Frank Polk]

Warsaw, June 17, 1919.

70. I have just returned from Vilna with Dr. Boris Bogen, director for Poland of the Jewish Joint Distribution Committee and [Lieut. Col.] Walter C. Bailey, director for Poland of the American Red Cross. We discussed with the local authorities and representatives of the Jewish colony the events which occurred at the time of the taking of the town and subsequently. Our impressions may be summarized as follows:

Vilna is a town of about 150,000 inhabitants of which 43 per cent are Jews. It was occupied by the Bolsheviki up to April 20th when it was taken by the Polish troops after street fighting. Order was not definitely established for three days when civil authority was taken over by Mr. [Bronisław] Piłsudski, the brother of the Chief of State, as District Commissioner.

The entire district in which Vilna is situated has suffered severely during the war, particularly during Bolshevik occupation. Food supplies now desperately short; the people in many villages being reduced to a point where they now have nothing to live on but soup made of nettles; their physical condition is very bad, typhus is generally prevalent. All semblance of governmental organization had disappeared during Bolshevik occupation and there was no recognized authority. The abnormal state of the population must be borne in mind in connection with what happened.

The events which involved the loss of Jewish lives took place during the capture of the town and the two days following during which time civil authority had not been established. In all 64 Jews were shot. The local authorities, military and civil, who were in Vilna at the time and immediately subsequent there to state that some of these people were killed during house to house fighting incident to the taking of the town. According to the statements of a representative Jewish informant the number thus killed was not more than 10. In other cases, where executions were carried out by military authorities there was in only a relatively small number of instances a regular court martial; in the others the justice was undoubtedly summary. The authorities justify the executions by the statement that some of these people were caught in active hostilities against the Polish troops, that others were shot for firing from windows, etc. In order to show that the streets during the period in question [omission].

The District Commissioner states that searches made in houses from which shots were believed to have been fired disclosed 24 machine guns and large quantity of rifles and hand grenades as well as much ammunition. This, he states, was sold to the Jews by Germans before they withdrew from Vilna. It is also stated that large numbers of Jews took part in the Bolshevik administration of the town and that many of them did not leave with the Bolsheviki; that there was an actively hostile provocative attitude on the part of the Jews on their arrival, and that the troops were bitter in their feeling against the Jews; and that this feeling was intensified by events in connection with the taking of the town. Members of the Jewish community stated that while it is true that a number of individual Jews did occupy [positions] under the Bolshevist administration this is also [true] of the Poles and White [i.e. Byelo] Russians and should not be especially charged up against the Jews. The members of the Jewish community also stated that their people did not engage in hostilities against Polish troops. They say, however, that the Bolsheviki were quartered in houses throughout the city and did undoubtedly shoot and throw hand grenades before escaping. The Jews state that about 2,000 of their number were arrested during the first few days, many of them sent to Lida and Bialystok. [Omission] being tense situation in the town they had no time for prolonged and careful investigation, that they gathered in all known Communists, every one in the houses from which shots had been fired or where concealed weapons had been found; also a large number of others were taken on suspicion, the authorities taking no chances. They state that almost immediately they began releasing those who were vouched for by responsible people and that within a short time a commision of Polish and Jewish members was established to investigate cases and release individuals. Representative Jews state that this commission [was] exceedingly slow and unsatisfactory in its work. Another commission was constituted and is now investigating cases. Nearly a thousand people are still under arrest in Vilna. The authorities state that persons now held are either known Communists or persons against whom there is such a strong presumption of guilt that they must be held for the present. Investigations continue, however, and liberations are being made from day to day.

The Jews also complain that many of their shops were pillaged, losses running into millions of marks. Pilsudski states in a [positive] manner that while there was looting of shops in a few cases, there was nothing general and that he has had no complaints of large losses although such complaints would in natural course come to his knowledge.

Our conclusions may be summarized as follows:

1. In view of the lack of any contemporary record we doubt whether the exact truth of [occurrences] can ever be ascertained.

2. The events described took place during the fighting of the first three days and before the authorities had obtained control.

3. At the time Polish troops entered Vilna there was such a wide spread feeling among the Polish population and among the soldiery against Jews believed to be allies of the Bolsheviki, war profiteers and enemies to Poland that a hostile sentiment prevailed against Jews as such.

4. On entering Vilna the troops were fired on from private houses throughout the town and some of these houses were occupied by Jews. Searches disclosed fuses, machine guns, and other weapons.

5. The troops during these three days made wholesale arrests, ransacked dwellings, and shops, and summarily executed a number of persons.

6. At the end of three days the military and civil authorities issued orders against pillaging and took effective control. Since that date no cases of serious violence are reported.

7. At the present time the laws so far as the protection [of] life is concerned are maintained.

8. The Jews are apprehensive; a general under current of anti-Jewish feeling still exists and gives cause for some concern.

9. The Jewish population expresses confidence in the fairness of the Chief of State, the Commissioner at Vilna and General [Stanisław Maria] Szeptycki commanding on the Bolshevik front.

Gibson

Source: F R, pp. 765—8.

Document No. 3

Letter, Gibson to William Phillips

Warsaw, July 6th, 1919

The Honorable William Phillips
The Assistant Secretary of State,
Washington

Dear Phillips:

Referring to my long letter today in regard to Jewish matters, I want to add a line as to the attitude of some American Jews.

As I have already said in several different ways, my one aim has been to discover some method by which we could help ameliorate the condition of the Jews in Poland. I have assumed that this was the aim of the American Jews who are carrying on the present agitation. I took it for granted that while they were acting on grossly exaggerated reports they were sincere and that discovery of their error would bring them relief and a welcome opportunity to tackle the problem itself rather than use up their energy in propaganda.

On arriving in Paris last week I was surprised to learn of the attack made upon me by Louis Marshall[2]; and still further surprised when I talked with him and other prominent Jews in Paris to observe that they seemed to be interested in the agitation for its own sake rather than in learning of the situation. They were outspokenly resentful of my having "destroyed the effect of months of Jewish work." Felix Frankfurter[3] insisted over and over that I "had no right" to make reports to the Department in regard to Jewish matters and should have "refused" on the ground that I could not possibly learn enough about them to make even general observations.

These gentlemen had accepted as gospel the whole fabric of truth and fiction from Jewish sources about events in Poland and I was supposed to swallow it whole as a basis for bluster and evasion. I finally took the offensive in the presence of witnesses and started through his interview in the *New York Times* of June 17th, checking off with a pencil each of his positive statements and showing it was false. I did not bore him by going all the way through this but stopped half way through to his manifest relief. At that time he had for several days had in his possession the telegram of Messrs. Schiff, Elkus, etc.[4], pointing out his injustice, but he had made no attempt on the strength of that telegram to ascertain the truth or make amends.

I was struck by the fact that these people did not want to discuss the situation or hear the views of an American representative who had just been in Poland. Their efforts were concentrated on an attempt to bully me into accepting the mixture of information and misinformation which they have adopted as the basis of their propaganda. On two occasions I brought out a file of my telegrams and asked them to point out to me the passages where I had made false statements or had been unfair. They took refuge behind the statement that I c o u l d n o t know anything about the subject and avoided specific objections save on two points.

(1) In a confidential telegram to the Department I had referred to a small criminal class of Jews as similar to the gunmen of New York. This was characterized as an attempt to stigmatize American Jews as gunmen.

(2) I telegraphed to the Department an order by General [Józef] Haller to his troops laying down the law concerning their treatment of the Jews. I suggested that this statement be given publicity and that I be furnished editorial comment for use here. This was described as Polish propaganda. I answered that if the Jews in America were anxious as to the safety of their co-religionists in Poland I should think they would be glad to learn of any measure taken on their behalf. As for the editorial comment, my idea was that if I could get the papers here to publish American comment approving General Haller's action it would encourage the authorities to go further along the same lines.

My statements on these matters were received with incredulity and manifest hostility, — but I was unable to elicit any other specific objections.

All this by way of preface.

I am still a good deal in the dark as to what this important group of American Jews wants. They made it clear to me that they do not care to have any diagnosis made that is not based entirely on Jewish statements as to conditions and events and does not accept them at face volue. If they are not ready to go into the question honestly I don't see how they can hope to accomplish anything for the good of their people. This is realized by intelligent Jews here who deplore the present propaganda which is made chielfy by American Jews. I am sorry to say that many people, among them some prominent Jews, feel that the whole movement is conducted without any regard for the welfare of the Jews in Poland, — that it has two principal directing forces:

(1) To weaken Poland in the interest of Germany who does not desire a formidable economic or political rival in the East; and

(2) A conscienceless and cold blooded plan to make the condition of the Jews in Poland so bad that they must turn to Zionism for relief.

The total result is not one that enhances American prestige.

Sincerely yours,

Hugh Gibson

Source: Gibson Papers, box 92.

Document No. 4

Report, Gibson to William Phillips

CONFIDENTIAL

Warsaw, July 6th, 1919

The Honorable William Phillips
The Assistant Secretary of State,
Washington.

Dear Phillips:

While I have wanted to send you a large amount of information concerning the Jewish position it has been difficult to get off more than our telegrams contained as we have not had a stenographer for weeks and have been snowed up with all sorts of other legation business. However here is a letter done on my own typewriter to give you some general ideas on the subject which may by useful.

When I came here I assumed it to be the desire of our Government to render any possible friendly service to prevent excesses or discrimination against the Jews. Consequently even before the Department first took the matter up I had given a large part of my time to the study of Jewish maters in general and made it my business to talk with all sorts of people, both Poles and Jews, with a view to finding how we might best contribute to alleviating the situation.

The Jewish question did not begin after the signature of the armistice. There is not a thing that happens today that does not have its roots in the old regime; and no true understanding can be based on separate examination of isolated events.

To begin with, the old Russian, German and Austrian Empires were the bulwark of such law and order as existed in this part of Europe. The system was rotten and oppressive and the Jews along with other minorities were subjected to hateful discriminations; public feeling was carefully aroused and maintained against the Jews as part of the system of dominating through internal dissension. On the other hand the Jews were spared actual physical violence except on those occasions when it suited the purposes of the authorities to let public feeling vent itself on them.

We have now overthrown the old system with its oppression. The legalized discrimination is gone. But we have not yet established a government with the virtues of the old regime and without its faults. The prejudices and hatreds have survived. For the present all we have done is to release a flood of pent up passion and hatred without establishing any strong authority to maintain even the degree of public order which prevailed before. The result is that while the legal discrimination and inequality have been removed and the Jews stand equal before the law theoretically, they have become a prey to physical violence to a degree that did not exist before.

The situation of the Jews in Poland is undoubtedly bad; not so much perhaps because of actual excesses as the inflamed feeling among Jews and Poles. Several hundred Jews have been killed since last November but when one remembers that are four millions of them in Poland, and when one bears in mind the upheavals through which the country has passed, and all the forces tending to create hatred of the Jews, this resolves itself into a mere symptom in the sickness of this part of the world. It is an alarming symptom, however, and requires immediate and earnest attention. The thing worries me is that as time goes on the state of public opinion is more and more aggravated against the Jews and a sane solution is being delayed by acrimonious discussion.

I notice that there is much confusion of terms in discussing this matter and that "massacre" and "pogrom" are used interchangeably. As a matter of fact the terms are not synonymous. A pogrom is some sort of organized mob violence against Jews as such, with destruction and theft of property. It may or may not entail physical violence or loss of life. In the strict understanding of the word the violence should be either abetted or countenanced by the authorities, but this seems to be ignored here, and both Poles and Jews refer to affairs as "pogroms" where it is admitted even by the victims that the authorities did their best to preserve order. Therefore you must be prepared to hear talk of pogroms and find in some instances that they amount to nothing more than the looting of a shop by a handful of peasants either before the police arrive on the scene or despite their efforts to prevent trouble. And after this has been talked about as a pogrom for a time it is likely to get into the headlines as a massacre. There is also careless use of the terms "atro-city", "looting", "pillage."

The anti-Jewish excesses seem to fall naturally into three categories:

(1). Popular outbreaks like the one at Lemberg [Lvov] in November when prejudice against the Jews was released by the complete collapse of the old forms of government before the Poles were able to set up any effective substitute for it.

(2). Events like those at Vilna, Lida and Pinsk which occurred during figthing against the Bolsheviki under abnormal conditions and intense suspicion against the Jewish population. In these instances although some Jews were killed in the ordinary course of street fighting by stray bullets, etc., most of them were executed by the military, usually without trial and with what was certainly summary justice.

(3). The general run of anti-Jewish outbreaks, the beating of Jews, cutting off beards, looting of shops. These are usually spontaneous outbursts of feeling arising from all sorts of causes, a street fight, a stray shot, a dispute with a Jew as to food prices, etc., etc.

First let me touch on the cases where Jewish lives have been taken in considerable numbers, — Lida, Vilna, Pinsk and Lemberg [Lvov]. In the agitation in America and England these affairs are referred to as massacres. As a matter of fact I should hesitate to describe them in that way without more evidence than I have thus far been able to secure. The loss of life occurred in each instance either during actual fighting while the town was being captured by the Polish armies or immediately thereafter before the Polish Government had been able to establish itself firmly in control. During the three days of fighting and disorder at Vilna while the Jewish dead numbered 64, the Polish soldiers killed numbered 34. There were a number of Polish civilian casualties as well. Some of the people at least were admittedly killed in the course of street fighting by stray bullets, etc. The rest were shot by military order and in some instances, no doubt by casual soldiers who afterwards justified their action by stating that the Jews in question were firing from windows or had committed some hostile act. How much foundation there was for this accusation in individual cases I have no way of knowing; but neither have the Jewish propagandists who simply denounce all the Polish sta-tements on the subject as falsehood without antything to support their view.

In each of these places the Polish authorities claim that the Jews were hostile: that they acted as spies for the enemy; that they had arms concealed in their houses; and that they fired from the windows on the Polish troops. The more temperate Jews deny that as a community they were hostile or committed any of the offenses referred to. They admit, however, that individuals undoubtedly did do these things. They also say that there was much firing from houses throughout the town but that the Jews themselves did not fire; that the houses were forcibly entered by Bolshevist or Ukrainian forces who fired upon the Polish troops and then retreated leaving the Jewish inhabitants of the houses to suffer the consequences. These same Jews say that the Poles are correct in saying that they found quantities of arms and machine guns in Jewish houses but they say that this was not with hostile intent against the Poles. I was told by Jews in Lida and Vilna that some of their co-religionists had bought these arms as an investment from the German troops before the withdrawal and that they were holding them for commercial purposes. However that may be, it certainly gave a color to Polish suspicions. It seems somewhat strange to me that the Bolchevists [sic] who wanted arms and munitions above everything, and who took them wherever they were to be found, should have left weapons in private hands unless satisfied as to the use to be made of them. In each of these instances the whole affair is a welter of uncertainty and positive statements and accusations on both sides, but I doubt whether the whole truth can be found out as to what hapened in any one place. The important thing to my mind is that the exesses took place during a time of high emotional stress, when suspicions ran high and when the Jews certainly laid themselves open to grave suspicions which may or may not have been justified. I have no doubt that innocent Jews were killed in the course of events at these various places but it must be remembered that innocent Poles were also shot and that Polish troops suffered considerable casualties.

In each of these places there was complaint of considerable looting of Jewish shops. I believe that there was some ground for these complaints but here again there is a broad margin of doubt as to what was looting for the purpose of hurting Jews, what was ransacking of shops and houses for the purpose of searching for arms, what was an attempt to secure foodstuffs which were needed for the troops and what was the general lawlessness that is likely to show itself at such a time. The authorities admit freely that a good deal of smashing and looting was done but emphatically deny the statements of the Jews as to the amount of their losses. In Vilna where the Jews constitute 43% of the population they own the greater part of the shops. For some time prior to the taking of the town by the Poles it had been in occupation of the Bolcheviki [sic] who had pretty well cleaned out the shops. In casual conversation the Jews complain that the Bolcheviki [sic] stripped the place. But when the time came to put in claims against the Poles over ten millions of marks were demanded from the Government. I did not have any time to go into the truth of these various claims but it is not in human nature not to make the best of an opportunity to get back bad losses and the chances are that the Polish authorities have some reason for saying that the loss of a few blankets and a sack of meal easily grew into thousands of marks of damage. This is just to show that it does not appear to be a simple clean-cut issue when you are on the ground.

One of the points which appeared to me to be very important was whether the Polish authorities had tolerated excesses against the Jews and I have taken every opportunity to inquire into this from the Jews themselves. In practically every instance I have been told that while the subordinate military authorities were arbitrary and sometimes brutal, the higher military and civil authorities as soon as they could be reached, did their best to stop all excesses. I say "in practically every instance" although the only exception was not altogether an exception. In Lemberg [Lvov] I was told by one of the leading Jews that he had gone to the Military Commander when the looting of the Jewish quarter began and had been told that the situation on the front was too precarious for any troops to be spared to put down the rioting in the town. At the time the Ukrainians had just been driven out and as fast as troops could be got into town over the one working railroad they were being hurried out to the east to try to consolidate the advantage that had been gained. I asked my informant whether he felt the commander's stand was well taken; and while he did so reluctantly, he said that the situation was undoubtedly very ticklish and that the difference of the troops necessary to restore order in the town might have turned the scales on the front.

So much for the incidents on the fighting front where Jews were killed. Other important affairs have taken place at Czestochowa and Cracow.

In the former place we again found quite abnormal conditions prevailing. There was a large and turbulent mining population for the most part unemployed and consequently highly sensitized for disorder of any sort. Czestochowa has for some time been a center for the smuggling of food from Poland into Germany and there is no getting away from the fact that Jews have figured prominently in this work. Members of our Relief Administration tell me that Jews have been picked up bearing passes from the German authorities authorizing them to cross the military lines "for the purpose of smuggling food". Food was scare in the town and prices high. Feeling was bitter against the Jews as it was felt that they were in some measure responsible for the shortage and consequent suffering. A trifling incident in which a shot was fired from a house by an unknown person and hit a young sodier was all that was needed to set the place ablaze. A crowd broke into the house from which they heard that the shot had been fired and dragged out a little Jew who more likely than not had nothing to do with the shooting. The police came to the rescue and one of the policemen was badly beaten in trying to protect him. A couple of soldiers were despatched [sic] to look for a doctor and came back with a Jewish barber surgeon. By that time excited people had passed round word of all sorts of dreadful things and when the doctor appeared between the two soldiers somebody called out that this was the man who did it and that he had grenades in his valise. The crowd without waiting to find out anything about it fell upon the little barber and killed him. Then a sailor in a German uniform who had not been seen in the place before spoke up and said that he would show them how to handle such matters and wound up with the cry: "Let's go to the markets." The crowd tore off in the wake of this trouble maker and smashed a lot of the booths mostly belonging to Jews and killed four more of them. Troops and police were called out and apparently every effort was made to afford proper protection to the Jews. Even the leaders of the Jewish community were willing to speak in high terms of the attitude of the authorities.

Later we had another incident at Cracow. It began with a row between a Jew peddler and a peasant woman as to the price of a scarf which the woman considered outrageous. Some of Haller's soldiers came along about this time and joined in. There were hot words which soon got to blows and the whole quarter was soon involved. There were casualties of all sorts, among them several soldiers and a French officer who was struck by a stray bullet. The authorities do not seem to have countenanced the disorders but they were undoubtedly weak in their handling of the situation and could have stopped the trouble much sooner with the display of more decision.

So much for the principal affairs on which complaint has been made.

There is much more complaint of minor persecution, the cutting and pulling of Jewish beards, insults, economic discrimination, etc. There is no doubt that a good deal of this sort of thing goes on but it is not a thing that can be stopped in a moment by governmental action. Back of this persecution is the situation which gives me the most concern and the one which I think gives most ground for activity on our part. I do not attach such vital importance to finding out whether 50 or 60 Jews were killed in a given place and who is responsible if we are to limit ourselves to finding these facts and let it go at that. If it is to be worth our while as Americans to mix into this matter it would seem to me that the thing to do is f i r s t to try to find out just what happened and then proceed to find out w h y it happened with a view in the end of discovering if possible some means of correcting the evil and preventing a recurrence of trouble in the future.

I have tried to look at the whole situation as a doctor would at a patient when called in to treat some troublesome illness. He has got to ask prying question, find out just how his patient has lived, what his excesses have been, what inherited or acquired ailments still poison his system. In no other way can he hope to make a diagnosis that will lead to a cure. Sometimes the patient resents questions which it is necessary to ask, sometimes he refuses to let you take his temperature or pulse and insists angrilly that you take his word for it. But if the doctor is any good he goes ahead and makes his diagnosis and tries to keep his patient as calm as possible. I have been in that rather thankless position in regard to this matter but have not felt that I could accept the word of anybody, Jew or Gentile, as to matters of controversy.

There are some inherited diseases handed down by the Russian and Austrian systems. The Russian was perhaps the worst and has left the most discouraging heritage. You know, of course, something of the old Russian discrimination against the Jew but I did not realize just how far it went until I came here. It was about as cold blooded and fiendish as anything you can imagine and has reduced large classes of the Jews to a state approaching that of the animal. By barring the Jews from higher education, professions and the army, and keeping them out of "Holy Russia" the old Russian Empire forced them into all sorts of crooked work and disreputable means of getting a livelihood. The fault for a great deal of what is happening now should properly be placed on the old Russian Government; but the people is not made up of philosophers, and when a Jew is caught as a food speculator or smuggler or receiver of stolen goods the crowd deals with him without any thought of the family of Romanoff. What is worse is that in the excitement of the moment they are quite as likely to kill or injure some perfectly innocent Jew. It is not justice and you sympathize with the Jews while realizing that by their actions they often goad the Poles to desperation. Everywhere you find the vicious circle which makes the whole problem so baffling.

There is no doubt that Jews control a great part of the food distribution and the food shops in the towns; that they use methods in handling these vitally important supplies that would cause riots in the United States on short notice. They are for the most part concentrated in the towns and make their living by handling the produce of the peasants in the surrounding country. Their methods seem to be pretty sharp and the peasant has no love for the Jew who is his only channel for disposing of his produce.

One outstanding fact is that there is no question of religious discrimination. I have not yet found anyone, Jew or Gentile, who felt that the religious consideration had any importance; — and I have asked pretty well everybody about the phase of the matter. In my telegrams I have gone pretty fully into the economic and social problems which are back of the whole question and there is not much use in elaborating on what I said there unless I can write a volume on the subject.

You may find some significance in the fact that Polish Jews are not nearly so active in this propaganda as their American and English, to say nothing of their German co-religionists. There is of course a violent Jewish press that is devoted chiefly to polemics against the Poles and the Polish Government, but decent and intelligent Jews deplore this attitude and constantly refer to it as being inspired wittingly or unwittingly by German influence. The best class of Jews are opposed to propaganda abroad and see that things have got to be changed here in the country before they can hope for better conditions. They say openly that the fault is not all on one side and that the Jews have also got to mend their ways. They resent this agitation abroad and are outspoken about it. You may have seen an interview which was telegraphed to the NEW YORK WORLD with Professor [Szymon] Askenazy [5] who characterizes the agitation by foreign Jews as harmful meddling. There are plenty more of the same sort and I am sure that some of our American Jewish agitators would be surprised at the sort of welcome they would receive from their co-religionists if they were to come here.

While we are criticizing the Poles for their behavior toward the Jews I feel that they have shown a good deal of self restraint in not showing up in the foreign press the fact that American boys in Haller's army have been among the worst offenders and that they have been a constant source of trouble. Before the Jewish question became acute here General Haller told me that he was greatly annoyed with his troops because they were violently anti-Semitic and that although he had given the strictest orders to keep them in line they were hounding Jews at every opportunity. He said they had never before seen the Orthodox Jew with his long beard and cloak, his greasy ringlets and none too cleanly appearance. When they heard the tales that the Polish peasants and townspeople had to tell about the profiteering and other offenses of the Jews their sense of justice was aroused and they set out to show "how the matter would be handled in America". Haller finally took such drastic measures that he seems to have got his men in hand and the amount of violence they do is reduced to a minimum. However, they are outspokenly anti-Jewish and I am not sure we have heard the last word from our own boys on the subject. To my mind it is not without significance that American boys should take this attitude.

One great difficulty is that some of the noisiest Jews in Poland and a good many outside have devoted themselves chiefly to destructive against the Polish State. This is foolish and hurts both races. When all is said and done they have much the same problems and the same interests. If, as the Jews say, the problem is chiefly economic, agitation that aggravates the economic situation of the country will not solve the problem. The thing for them to do is to help lift up Poland and lift their own people along with the country. It's the only way that will get any lasting results. I feel that we can render good service in helping to bring Poles and Jews together for discussion and constructive work. But such service on our part is delayed and hampered by the attempt of American Jews to hurt Poland in the eyes of the world.

I feel very strongly that propaganda is fraught with grave danger for the Jews. If carried on in its present scale with its present violent character it is quite conceivable that it will succeed in prejudicing public opinion to such a point as to damage Poland in some specific way. She may be refused a foreign loan as a protest against her treatment of the Jews; she may be refused some given frontier on the ground that she is not fit to rule over minorities. The Jews in Poland have had little to do with this agitation abroad but when the time comes that Poland suffers as a result of it, the whole thing will doubtless be wrongly attributed to the Jews of the country. And if the people in their resentment do rise up and massacre Jews on a scale never before known, the blood guilt will be on the foreign Jews who with wicked disregard of the facts or the danger to human lives have played with this tremendously delicate situation. I have very frankly stated my views on this question to the group of American Jews in Paris and I should like to put my observation on record.

I have no desire to whitewash the Polish Government as some of the American Jews have alleged. Nobody sees better than I do its shortcomings or has been more outspoken in upbraiding it. The Polish Government has not yet got its footing in authority and is slow and sometimes timid in action. I have made the Government's life a burden by hammering on the Jewish question morning, noon and night. As to the question itself I have found no disagreement or opposition. The people in the Government realize the gravity of the question and want to find some solution for it. They recognize the friendly nature of our interest in the matter and are surprisingly open to suggestions. The only trouble is that the machinery of government has not reached a pitch of efficiency and everybody is still inclined to put things off. We play the ungrateful part of a persistent friend and keep pushing until action is taken. The strict orders by General Haller and the Minister of the Interior and of War are the direct result of our activity. The right sentiments were there but it took a lot of pushing to get them expressed in the proper terms, and unfortunately a ministerial proclamation does not become instantaneously effective in every outlying village.

In attempting to obtain results in this question the ineffectiveness of the Polish Government in every department must be recognized. It must be remembered that men with any experience in government affairs do not exist in numbers adequate to the needs. The result is that a foreign representative here can obtain a hearing, is met with sympathy and receives well intended promises. Then nothing happens. Bad faith is not the explanation, for as often as not the affair is a matter in which obvious Polish interests are concerned. The explanation is rather that the governmental machine does not yet function well. I have not spared them in my comments on several episodes where the neglect or indifference of some functionary was revealed; and the new acting head of the Foreign Office and his principal assistant now eat and sleep there in an effort to stimulate the energy of the place. And yet I could cite repeated instances of recent failures. For instance the Legation was informed a week ago in writing by an important Foreign Office official that food shipmentes from Danzig had been stopped by the Germans, and that Warsaw had food for only three days. We stayed up half the night and put our modest machinery at work to check up the statement. It was quite incorrect. Warsaw had food for eleven days and four more trains came in that night. The train service had at no time been interrupted but the Ministry for Foreign Affairs had neither the intelligence nor the energy to obtain the information needed and depended on Allied assistance to do it. I deplore the weakness of this government but I see nothing to replace it. A more radical government would only add to the chaos already existing. Is it not our task to be patient and to try to train and mould the material which is at hand so long as its good intentions are manifest?

In the Jewish problem there are influential Polish fanatics, usually of the [Roman] Dmowski following. The latter's short-sighted policies have been manifest many times in the past, and I think it is questionable whether, good Pole as he is, he does not at every turn injure his country much more than he helps it. A member of the Committee on Foreign Affairs, the Reverend Mr. [Kazimierz] Lutosławski [6], told a member of the Legation that there is not a single Jew in the country who is a good citizen of Poland. Such a statement is absurd on its face, but it is clear that the path of the government is not always smooth when it has minds of this sort to deal with in the Diet. This country is not unique in having a large percentage of the population who are governed by what they read in the papers, and the press is woefully low in its standards. To certain editors every Jew is an enemy — Bolchevik [sic] or German — every ungrateful influence or event is attributed to Jewish intrigue. That is why I have asked occasionally for editorial comment from the United States, in order to inject some leaven into this mass. I think the tone of the press is becoming slowly better — but if the American Jews would concentrate their attention on such real offenders as the "Gazeta Warszawska" instead of on Poland and Poles "as such" they would be really helping to remedy the situation.

To sum up this long dissertation which has rather run away with me — the problem is one of the most complicated and delicate in all this complex European situation. It is not a thing that can be conjured by a formula or regulated by legislation imposed by foreign governments. Some obvious things can be done and are being done to improve the situation. But the greatest good and the only real hope for Poles and Jews lies in educational work of many sorts. Anything approaching a solution will require all the patience and combined intelligence of as many sane people as can be induced to tackle the question. Much good can be done with common sense and hard work — much harm by irresponsible slap dash methods. We must not fear to tread but for Heaven's sake let's try to keep the fools from rushing in.

Sincerely,

Hugh Gibson

Source: Gibson Papers, box 92.

Letter, Louirs Marshall to Abram I. Elkus

August 19, 1919

I am returning to you the letter of Gibson to Phillips [7] which you were so kind as to send me, together with the letter from Phillips to you enclosing it.

I have read what Gibson has said with great care. There is much that is admirable in his comments, but there is more that is inaccurate and ill-digested. Everybody knows what a pogrom is. There is no necessity of going into a learned discussion as to its meaning or derivation. When there is a manifest disposition in one part of the population of a country or a city to visit upon another their hatred and prejudice by means of murder, pillage and the infliction of indignities, it is a pogrom. If these manifestations occur, not in isolated instances or sporadically, but frequently in different parts of a country, all of the same general character, there can be no doubt that they are either sanctioned by those in power or are regarded as of insufficient importance to make it worth while to punish the perpetrators. The evidence that there have been frequent manifestations of this character in Poland since the armistice, without going back further, is convincing. The various messages sent by Mr. Gibson to the State Department, which were communicated to me in Paris by Mr. Grew [8], and the authentic reports that I have received from various parts of Poland, demonstrate this.

I make this statement in the interest of historic accuracy, and not for the purpose of entering upon a controversy. It is my sincere hope, now that Poland has ratified the treaty of June 28, 1919, wherein she undertook to protect racial, religious and linguistic minorities, that a brighter future will dawn and that all of the unhappy experiences of the past may be forgotten. Speaking, therefore, solely for the purpose of avoiding a tacit admission of the correctness of Mr. Gibson's statements, I make the following comments.

(1) He refers to the occurrence at Lemberg [Lvov] as due to a collapse of the old forms of government before the Poles were able to set up any effective substitute for it. The difficulty at Lemberg was that the Poles killed the Jews, that their military commanders did nothing to prevent the atrocities which were committed, and that the officer who should have been held responsible was subsequently promoted.

(2) The killing of the Jews in Wilna [Vilna], Lida and Pinsk is said to have occurred during fighting against the Bolsheviki. As a matter of fact there was no fighting against the Bolsheviki at Pinsk at all when the thirty-seven unarmed and unoffending Jews were arrested, and without a trial were executed by an officer who had, a month before, soid to Mr. Brailsford, an eminent English journalist, that one Jew in every ten should be killed. At the time when the Jews were killed at Wilna [Vilna] and Lida fighting against the Bolsheviki had ceased, and most of the Jews who were killed at Wilna [Vilna] were slaughtered at points remote from those where there had been fighting against the Bolsheviki.

(3) Mr. Gibson admits that most of the Jews in these towns "were executed by the military, usually without trial", and then he concludes with the extraordinary statement that this was "certainly summary justice." The abuse of the word "justice" in this connection is rather abhorrent to one whose conception of justice involves as an essential element the idea that execution without trial is murder, and not justice. The men who were killed at Pinsk were entirely innocent of any offense which warranted even arrest; and the same is true of the Jews who were killed at Wilna [Vilna] and Lida.

(4) He then speaks of the general run of anti-Jewish outbreaks, which consists of the beating of Jews, the cutting off of beards, the looting of shops. They are characterized as "spontaneous outbursts of feeling arising from all sorts of causes." Those familiar with conditions know that there is no spontaneity in these attacks. They are deliberate, continuous, and unrelenting. These acts have been so persistent that General Pilsudski, General Haller and the Polish Diet found it necessary to protest against these atrocities, which they very properly referred to as persecutions. They do not result from street fights or disputes as to food prices. Men walking peacefully upon the street, entering railroad stations, traveling on trains are beaten and their beards are not only cut off, but they are pulled out with the adherent skin.

So much for Mr. Gibson's classification of what he calls "anti-Jewish excesses," employing the term now adopted by the Poles. I am at a loss to understand why "excesses" of the character described are more amiable exhibitions of brutality than pogroms, atrocities or massacres.

(5) Mr. Gibson finds fault that, in the agitation in America and England, these affairs are referred to as massacres. He hesitates to use that term because the loss of life occurred in each instance either during actual fighting while the town was being captured by the Polish armies or immediately thereafter before the Polish Government had been able to establish itself firmly in control. He forgets that at Pinsk the "massacres" were perpetrated by the officer in command of the Polish garnison. The Polish Government was firmly established. I have already referred to the fact that at Wilna [Vilna] the Jews were killed after the Poles had established themselves in control.

I would like to have Mr. Phillips read the account that appeared within the past few days in The Forward written by Mr. Abraham Cahan, who spent eighteen days in Wilna [Vilna] and who properly entitles the article "Eighteen Days in Hell." Mr. Cahan went to Poland against my wishes and at the express instance of Commander Baker, one of Mr. [Herbert] Hoover's aids. His evidence is therefore certainly entitled to the most favorable consideration. I enclose copies of the articles which can doubtless be translated for Mr. Phillips in the State Department.

(6) I cannot say that I feel impressed by the fairness of Mr. Gibson's statement that the Jews laid themselves open to grave suspicions in Lida and Wilna [Vilna] which may or may not have been justified. They were either justified or they were not. They cannot have been both. When one considers that, at Wilna [Vilna], not only were men and women and children killed, but property of the value of millions of Marks was carried away, this talk of the Jews laying themselves open to suspicion is unfair, to say the least.

(7) He then adds that he has no doubt that innocent Jews were killed in the course of events at these various places. He might have expressed himself with greater certainty. But why should he have added that it must be remembered that innocent Poles were also shot and that Polish troops suffered considerable casualties. It is not pretended that the Jews attacked their Polish neighbors or fought against the Polish troops. They were not engaged in pillaging the property of their neighbors or in attacking them.

I resent the innuendoes with which Mr. Gibson's letter is replete.

(8) Again, although he admits that there was ground for the complaints of the looting of the Jewish shops, he is so charitable as to express the belief that there is "a broad margin of doubt as to what was looting for the purpose of hunting Jews, what was ransacking of houses

and shops for the purpose of searching for arms, what was an attempt to secure foodstuffs which were needed for the troops and what was the general lawlessness that is likely to show itself at such a time." What does he mean by "looting for the purpose of hunting Jews"? There is no doubt that Jews were hunted and that their property was looted. The combination is a novelty to me.

(9) His statement that the claims made for reparation were excessive in amount is entirely beside the question. Mr. Gibson says that the authorities admit freely that a good deal of smashing and looting was done. That is the important proposition. Whether the losses amounted to 5,000,000 Marks or 10,000,000 Marks is of secondary importance. His insinuation that "it is not in human nature not to make the best of an opportunity to get back bad losses," is an unworthy one, especially in view of the fact that he says that he did not have time to investigate the truth of these various claims. Then why should he express any opinion on the subject in the absence of evidence, and accept the statement of Polish authorities "that the loss of a few blankets and a sack of meal easily grew into thousands of Marks of damage"? I suppose that he would also have accepted the explanation of the authorities of Pinsk with respect to the seizure of 100,000 Marks sent by the Joint Distribution Committee to that city for the purpose of feeding the starving Jews of that locality after the murders had been committed there by the military authorities, and yet, after waiting more than three months, the money was at last returned, but only after repeated and insistent demands and after the fact of this extraordinary seizure had received publicity.

(10) The statement as to what occurred at Czenstochova [Częstochowa] does not conform to the reports which I received in Paris. But assuming that the occurrence originated in the manner indicated and detailed by Mr. Gibson, it proves that the attack on the Jews was a murderous one. The fact that Jews were charged with smuggling food into Germany does not amount to either a palliation or extenuation of what took place. The smuggling of food was either a crime against the laws of Poland or, so far as the law is concerned, an innocent act. If it was a crime and the Jews were guilty of it, they should have been proceeded against by means of legal process. The fact that they were not proceeded against gives rise to the presumption that the acts complained of were either not unlawful or that there was no evidence to show that the Jews were guilty of those acts. One might as well justify a mob, partly civilian and partly military, in killing men, women and children indiscriminately here in New York, or anywhere else in the United States, because profiteering has taken place. It is not even pretended that the Jews who were killed were themselves engaged in

smuggling or profiteering. It is sad to find in the report of an American Minister an attempt to minimize a dreadful massacre by such insinuations as those which Mr. Gibson has made.

(11) The incident at Cracow receives but slight consideration in Mr. Gibson's letter. Apparently he would have it appear that it was a negligible occurrence. As a mater of fact the number of those who were seriously injured was in the neighborhood of 100, as I now recollect the figures. The very fact that General Haller found it necessary on account of this occurrence among others, to reprimand his soldiers, shows that it could not have been an unimportant occurrence.

(12) I am, however, more astounded by what Mr. Gibson says of complaints of what he calls "minor persecution" — the cutting and pulling of beards, insults, and economic discrimination. He admits that there is no doubt that much of "this sort of thing" is going on. He adds that it cannot be stopped in a moment by governmental action. To my mind this persecution is infinitely worse in its aggregate effect than the killing of 100 or 500 men. It is the humiliation which is practiced relentlessly and continuously that tells and that results in the degradation of those who are the victims of it. To meet death would be preferable to such treatment as that which is accorded to respectable and venerable men, to industrious and self-respecting merchants and workmen.

The economic discrimination to which reference is made is the boycott which Mr. Dmowski admitted to me was deliberately initiated by him for the purpose of destroying the Jews of Poland. In October last I asked Mr. Dmowski to put an end to this boycott which he admitted was still in force. He said that if he attempted to do so the members of his political party would say that he had been bought. In November, 1918, in company with Judge Mack, Oscar S. Strauss, Rev. Dr. Stephen S. Wise and Mr. Jacob de Haas, I asked Messrs. Dmowski and Paderewski to take action which would end this boycott.[9] While the former admitted that it was in force and that he was responsible for it, Mr. Paderewski met the admission with the remark "Mr. Dmowski, you are flattering yourself," and claimed that the boycott had practically ceased. It has not ceased, and at this very moment the Polish Government is making discrimination against the Jews in respect to the allotment of supplies and raw materials. While it may be conceded that such acts cannot be stopped "in a moment" by governmental action, there has been no attempt to stop the boycott by governmental action. On the contrary, much of the discrimination which now exists is the result of governmental action.

(13) After very properly referring to conditions in Poland as "inherited diseases" contracted under the Russian and Austrian systems, which are characterized as "about as cold-blooded and fiendish as

anything you can imagine," he balances that statement with the remark that "there is no doubt that Jews control a great part of the food distribution and the food shops in the towns and use methods in handling these supplies that would cause riots in the United States on short notice". As a matter of fact the Jews do not control the food distribution. The great landowners, who control the production of food in Poland, belong to the nobility. They are not Jews. They take advantage of existing conditions by raising the price of foodstuffs, which they sell through middlemen to the small dealers. The prices which the latter charge are greatly enhanced by the profiteering of the producers. While there are Jews who conduct little food shops and have stalls at the markets, their part of the bussiness of food distribution constitutes but a very small percentage of the total business transacted.

The statements that have been recently made by Attorney General [Mitchell] Palmer, the facts which come under the observation of every householder in America, show that conditions exist here in the United States in respect to profiteering on food which are infinitely less excusable than those to which Mr. Gibson directs attention, and yet no riots have occurred here. It is so natural, however, for one who comes in social contact with the natural enemy of the Jew and who gives the subject merely superficial attention, to accept the point of view which makes the Jew the convenient scapegoat for all of the sins that have been inherited from the past and for all the misdeeds and incompetency of those in power, that I am not surprised that Mr. Gibson has fallen into the old rut.

(14) I come now to a portion of Mr. Gibson's letter which I regard as inexcusable and as positively insulting to the Jews of America and of England. He says that the Polish Jews are not nearly so active in the propaganda with respect to the treatment accorded to them as are their American and English correligionists, that the best class of Jews in Poland are opposed to propaganda abroad and resent this agitation. He feels "that we can render good service in helping to bring the Poles and Jews together for discussion and constructive work. But such service on our part is delayed and hampered by the attempt of American Jews to hurt Poland in the eyes of the world."

I am astounded at these expressions. The Jews of Poland were without food, without shelter, without clothing, and at the same time were victims of the boycott and of these exhibitions of hatred and animosity, of humiliation and cruelty, as admitted by Mr. Gibson. In their distress they cried out to their coreligionists of England and, especially, of America to help them in their misery. They were so poverty-stricken that they could not help each other adequately. They could get no assistance from the Government. It therefore became a duty, based on the simplest dictates of humanity, that the Jews of America should come to the rescue. They did so with the sanction and the assistance and sympathy of our State Department and of every branch of our Government. Much of the food that was sent to Poland by the Jews of America was distributed without regard to sectarian lines, to non-Jews as well as to Jews. When the news came to America that these massacres occurred at Lemberg [Lvov], Pinsk, Lida, Wilna [Vilna], Cracow and Chenstochovo [Częstochowa], and many other localities, that the Jews were subjected to this humiliation and to these indignities that have been described, that the economic discrimination which had been going on for seven years was still continuing, when the cry of anguish of their coreligionists reached their ears, what could the Jews of America have done but to protest, to give publicity to these awful occurrences, to ask for the intervention of the civilized Governments of the world to put an end to these monstrous brutalities? According to Mr. Gibson, the Christian world should have remained silent when it learned of the Armenian massacres, for fear that the Turks might be aroused to further resentment, and, to quote Mr. Gibson, "the people in their resentment might rise up and massacre Jews (Armenians) on a scale never before known." What would have been said if you, for instance, Mr. Elkus, had argued that the Christian community of the United States should not protest against the Turkish atrocities lest "the blood guilt would be on the foreign Chrisians who with wicked disregard of the facts or the danger to human lives have played with this tremendously delicate situation"? I am inclined to believe that your resignation would have been requested in fifteen minutes. To your lasting honor, however, be it said that you raised your voice, not in favor of the brutes who massacred the Armenians, but in the cause of a common humanity, and that your voice rang forth eloquently throughout our country in protest against these nefarious practices, these massacres.

Is it possible that Mr. Gibson refers to the fact that American and English Jews were active in the endeavor to procure for the racial, religious and linguistic minorities of Poland and other of the European countries guaranties of civil, religious and political rights, and that the majorities in these countries resent this action as interference? Then, if that is the case, it might be well form him to go higher up in placing responsibility for the massacres of Jews which he predicts "on a scale never before known." The plea for emancipation, for equality before the law, for according the rights of citizenship, received the approval of the Peace Conference and of the great leaders who made the plea effective. When Greece fought for her freedom and independence our country did not hesitate to express its approval of the aspirations of that patriotic people. When Hungary sought independence America sympathized with her. When Poland sought to break the chains which bound her to Prussia and Austria the American people did not hesitate to express their friendship. And yet an American Minister ventures to threaten American Jews with responsibility for murders to be committed by the Poles because of their efforts to ameliorate the condition of their brethren.

As one who has taken an active part in this movement, I can say that I would personally rather die ten thousand deaths than to have been guilty of the crime of being silent in the face of the wrongs which my brethren have suffered in Poland and other East European States. If it should happen that, in consequence of what has been done, thousands of Polish Jews shall be murdered by their fellow-citizens, I shall not feel the slightest responsibility, and if I had known in advance that they would be murdered I should not have been silent. Far better that they should die as freemen than be degraded as they have been in the past, and as Mr. Gibson admits they are being degraded and humiliated at the present time. There is not a Jew in Poland who has the slightest self-respect, who has not prayed for the dawn of emancipation, who has not rejoiced at what the Peace Conference has done, and who is not willing to die for the rights which have been secured to him. The Jews whom Mr. Gibson quotes and whom he has elsewhere described as assimilationists, are few in number and are either apostates or renegades, who are merely considering their private interests by those whom they have not sought to help, though they were able to do so. Some of them were in the employ of the Polish Government at Paris and were paraded there as spokesmen of Jews who were entirely satisfied with prevailing conditions. That fact in itself, in the light of Mr. Gibson's admissions, enables one to appreciate the value of their testimony.

Let me, however, say that the Jews of America and of England who have fought for the rights and for the protection desirability of coming to an understanding with the Poles and of cultivating friendly relations with them. As soon as the treaty with Poland was signed at Versailles, as the President of the Committee of the Jewish Delegations at Paris and acting under a resolution unanimously adopted by the members of that Committee, who came from all parts of Europe and America, I called on Mr. [Ignacy] Paderewski, by appointment, in company with Mr. [Nahum] Sokolov [10], a native of Poland an a man of great distinction. We congratulated Poland, through him, on the reattainment of her sovereignty. We expressed our gratification at the action taken by Poland evidenced by the signature of the treaty looking to the grant of equal rights to all minorities in that country. He expressed himself as greatly pleased by what we had said. We then discussed with him frankly the subject of Jewish persecution. He expressed his regret at what had occurred and stated that he would take immediate action to prevent the recurrence of the conditions of which we had complained, We then stated that it was the desire of every Jew in Poland to be helpful to the Government of hich he now formed a part, to aid in the development of Poland's resources, to prove what patriotic devotion to her interests by all of her citivens could accomplish, and that it only depended upon the majority to utilize the energies and the good-will of the Jewish population by giving them in fact as well as in theory that equality which the Polish treaty guaranteed. We called attention to what the Jews who had been driven from the Polish territory as the result of Czaristic brutality, had accomplished in the United States and what they had added to the national life and to the spiritual forces in operation here. Mr. Paderewski requested us to reduce to writing what we had said, because he desired to make use of it in the addresses which he intended to deliver before the Polish Diet and before the army, and generally on his return to Poland, which he expected would occur shortly thereafter. We did so. I am informed that he carried out his purpose. The fact that the Polish Diet confirmed the treaty according minority rights by a vote, as reported in the newspapers, of 245 to 41, shows that what was said made some impression. We have also written to the Jews of Poland on the same lines, stating, in substance, now that they have been secured the rights of citizenship we were certain that they would give to Poland the full measure of devotion and that their effort would be to aid in the development of what was now their country. That is the attitude which has been publicly taken by every influential Jew in America and in Europe, and that will continue to be their policy. If, however, the persecution of the Jews in Poland shall continue, I can say without the slightest hesitation that the Jews of America and of England will continue to protest and to use every ounce of their power in presenting the facts to the world, so that its conscience may be aroused. I hope that it will be unnecessary. I have not heard of any further massacre since the signature of the Treaty of Versailles and since the protests of American and English Jewry were heard throughout the world.

(15) Mr. Gibson praises the Poles for their self-restraint "in not showing up in the foreign press the fact that American boys in Haller's army have been among the worst offenders and that they have been a constant source of trouble." Although I took an active part in assisting in the raising of our conscript army, I am not a military man, but I cannot understand how it is possible for soldiers in the ranks to be guilty of the offenses, the commission of which by his soldiers General Haller admits, without grave reflection on those in command. When I consider that General Haller has the manhood to state that he was greatly annoyed with his troops because they were violently anti-Semitic

and that in spite of his orders to keep them in line they were hounding Jews at every opportunity, I am at a loss to understand the tenderness which Mr. Gibson throughout his letter exhibits toward those guilty of these outbreaks of anti-Semitism. Mr. Gibson says that to his mind it is not without significance that American boys should take this attitude. Neither is it to mine. During the time that recruiting was done at Pittsburgh for Haller's army, my attention was called to the fact by Mr. A. Leo Weil, one of the leading lawyers of that city, that one of the recruiting officers, in order to induce Poles to enlist under the Haller flag, told them that there would be opportunities to get even with the Jews, and other similar arguments were used which I will not undertake to quote because the documents are not now readily accesible to me. Although Mr. Weil and I made this the subject of complaint to Washington, by the time that the investigation could be made memories had weakened and a Scotch verdict was rendered. I am satisfied, however, that this was not an isolated instance when an attempt was made to instill anti-Semitic prejudice into the minds of young Amercans who were invited to fight in Poland. The existence of that anti-Semitism in Haller's army, as admitted by him, is in itself a sufficient explanation of the dissemination of the virus among those coming from America. The very suggestion that this hounding of the Jews was due to the fact that the American soldiers had never before seen the Orthodox Jew "with his long beard and cloak, his greasy ringlets and none too cleanly appearance", is disgraceful. I have no fear of what these returning soldiers may do in America. I rely on the record made by the 175,000 Jews who entered the American army and navy during the war and on the appreciation of our fellow-citizens of what they accomplished.

(16) Mr. Gibson intimated that the Jews have devoted themselves chiefly to destructive criticism against the Polish State. This is not the fact. They have merely criticized abuses. They have pointed out the suffering which they have endured in consequence of the economic boycott. Their struggle has been for liberty, for equality, for fraternity. They have clamored for the right to render service for their country. Hitherto they have been prevented. Up to the present moment they are still discriminated against commercially and economically. There is a very simple way by which Poland can gain the love of every part of her population, and that is, by obliterating the animosity which has existed on the part of the majority against the minority, by putting an end to anti-Semitism, by regarding the Polish citizen of the Jewish race and faith as entitled to the same rights as those of any other race or creed in Poland.

There is much more that I might add, but Mr. Gibson's long dissertation has, to use his expression, likewise "run away with me."

I would feel derelict in my duty if I permitted what he has said to go unanswered. I trust, therefore, that you will communicate my views to Mr. Phillips. I should be very glad indeed if what I have said were submitted to Mr. Gibson. When I met him in Paris I spoke to him along these lines and gave him every assurance that it was the policy of the Jews to make friends with the Poles, and that it depended entirely upon the Poles as to whether or not they would take advantage of the industry and energy and the ability of their Jewish fellow-citizens. We were to have further conversation on the subject, but before we could resume it he was obliged to return to Warsaw. I was satisfied that whatever information he received was solely from a single source and that his views were extremely one-sided. I am more convinced than ever that this has been his difficulty. It has been easier for him to converse with Polish officialdom than with those who have been the victims of that anti-Semitism which he recognizes but at the same time seeks in a sense to excuse.

[Louis Marshall]

Source: Louis Marshall. *Champion of Liberty. Selected Papers and Addresses*, Charles Reznikoff, ed., Philadelphia: The Jewish Publication Society of America, 1957, Vol. 2, pp. 1—11.

Document No. 6

Letter, Gibson to Robert Lansing

Warsaw, February 14, 1920.

The Honorable Robert Lansing,
Secretary of State,
Washington, D. C.

Dear Mr. Secretary:

Indications are not lacking that the Jewish question in Poland is looming up again somewhat as it did at this time last year.

There are two phases of this matter which appear worthy of consideration:

(a) This recurrent agitation appears to be almost entirely in the hands of American Jews.

(b) The resentment aroused by these machinations may lead to fresh trouble.

As the first of these considerations is contributing to the danger indicated by the second, I feel that we have a direct concern in this whole situation and I therefore venture to lay before you a general expression of my views.

Last year's campaign which was based entirely on pogroms and outrages upon the Jews was conducted chiefly by American Jews and in large measure through the representatives in Poland of the Jewish Joint Distribution Committee, which ostensibly is here purely for relief work and should not concern itself with other affairs. The agitation was so characterized by gross exaggeration that although it had a momentary success it was eventually discredited when the truth became known. The attacks upon Poland were abandoned with bad grace and I have throughout been of the opinion that the individuals behind the movement were merely awaiting a more favorable opportunity to resume their anti-Polish activities.

I am inclined to believe that there will be no attempt to revive the campaign upon the basis of what has happened in Poland for there is little chance of getting general credence for the stories that were disproved last year. As a matter of fact, enough dreadful things did happen to the Jews in Poland to have made a very bad impression if the truth had been told about them; but it was not.

I think there may be several schemes under consideration: one of them to develop the present campaign about massacres of Jews in the Ukraine with a consistent endeavor to confuse that country and Poland so far as possible in the public mind. I am inclined to think that there is an alternative plan of withdrawing the entire force of Jewish relief workers and returning to the United States with a statement that they were driven out by Polish persecution and had to abandon their humanitarian work. There are various independent agitations but the foregoing will indicate two possible lines of action which will bear watching.

I am convinced that the group which has carried on the anti-Polish agitation is not representative of American Jewry. The individuals most directly concerned are deliberately misrepresenting the situation. On the other hand, I am sure the vast majority of American Jews are merely misled and sincerely desirous of helping their co-religionists in Central Europe. As matters are developing now, they stand to do much more harm than good and if in their ignorance the present campaign of international intrigue continues to receive their misguided support, we must frankly anticipate the growth of anti-Jewish feeling in the United States.

I think we should bear in mind as of special significance the fact that at no time have the Jews of Poland taken any considerable part in the anti-Polish agitation. The great majority with whom I have talked feel that positive harm has been done them by the campaign waged abroad, supposedly in their behalf. Some of the ignorant Jews have doubtless lent themselves to the leaders of American agitation, but the better-class Jews whom I know are frankly resentful at what they termed "the meddlesomeness of foreigners", who have not consulted the wishes of Polish Jewry and are inspired chiefly by selfish motives of promoting their own ends.

It is clear that much resentment has been caused among the Poles by the agitation abroad, and the unfortunate part of it is that only those who are particularly well informed realize how little the Jews of Poland are responsible. The more intelligent Jews not only deplore the needless resentment which has been caused but feel that more serious consequences may be feared for the future. Poland is passing through what may be the most crucial moment in her history. At such a time as this feelings always run high and it is to be feared that if Poland suffers any misfortune which can possibly be ascribed to the influence or intrigue of the Jews, popular resentment will be visited not upon the foreign agitators but upon individual Jews who, for the most part, could in the nature of things have had nothing to do with the matter. I tried to impress this idea upon Mr. Louis Marshall and other American Jews. when I was in Paris last June in the belief that no fair-minded man would carry on agitation of this sort in the knowledge that it would react upon the lives of innocent people who were unable to defend themselves.

Even this risk might be justifiable if there were any great and good end to be gained. I have raised this question in conversation with most of the American Jews who have come to this country and have thus far been unable to discover anything beyond a desire either for agitation for its own sake or to punish Poland as a whole for what has happened to the Jews, or in some cases a definite idea of making her economic and political situation as difficult as possible. The nearest approach to a constructive idea was that enunciated by an American Jew, to the effect that if Poland were to be sufficiently intimidated through propaganda, she would submit to any conditions imposed upon her in the interest of the Jews, in order to stop the campaign and get assurances of foreign loans, etc.

The present situation can be briefly stated. The so-called Jewish situation question is entirely social and economic. I have not yet found a Polish Jew who feels that the question is religious in character. In the words of Dmowski, "there are not enough bread-crumbs to go around." Somebody in the nature of things must go without and as the Jew is economically the weaker, he is the one who does not get his share. This discrimination is made easier by the fact that troughout the centuries of his life in Poland, he has jealously maintained his separation and his distinctive dress and language, which he often speaks to the exclusion of Polish. This tends to make him conspicuous and different from other members of the community, and there is nothing more calculated than such outward differences to keep alive jealousy and resentment.

The one thing calculated to make the life of the Jew less intolerable is to improve his economic condition. Here the fallacy of the present policy of agitation becomes clear. If Poland is weakened politically and economically, this cannot help but have a disastrous effect on the Jews. The only possible way to improve their condition is to improve the general condition of the country itself. The Jews are practically all engaged as middlemen and in petty trade of one sort or another entirely dependent upon the prosperity of the community. There is not now enough of this business to support several millions of people with a minimum of comfort that is essential to self-respect. If, on the other hand, Poland becomes prosperous, the body of Jews in Poland will be lifted on the rising tide of prosperity.

I believe that the best American Jews are really actuated by a desire to help their co-religionists in this country. Such people could do a great constructive work if they would silence the people who are inspired only by blind hatred and a desire to intrigue and would set to work to improve economic conditions.

Quite aside from the general question of the welfare of the Jews, I feel gravely apprehensive about the continued political intrigue of American citizens against a friendly Government. If this goes on unchecked, the possible consequences are obvious, and if we are involved in embarrassing international difficulties which arouse widespread resentment, it is readily conceivable that the Jewish community in America, whether they have been collectively responsible or not, will have to bear a heavy burden of suspicion and resentment. It seems to me that the time has nearly come to lay some of these considerations before the leading American Jews who, if they understand the situation, cannot but feel the same as any other patriotic American. I am sure that they would realize the folly of trying to improve the already precarious situation of the Jews in Poland by destroying the only source of their livelihood and that they would feel shamed as I do by the scandalous behavior of American Jews in Poland. If they exercise their authority to suppress improper activities and work constructively, their efforts would be a decided national asset, and I feel that we should support them to the limit of our strength.

There is no doubt that the Jew in Poland does have a hard time and where an individual Jew acts straightforwardly, I instinctively make a little greater effort on his behalf than I do for anyone else; it is merely the natural impulse of any decent man to help out the man who is working under difficulties. I must say, however, that in the case of most of the American Jews who have come over here, their behavior has been such as to make it extremely difficult for us to help them. There have been conspicuous exceptions, like Dr. Boris Bogen and Dr. Isidore Hirschfield [11], who have accomplished most valuable work.

Perhaps the most effective action that could be taken would be a radical change in the personnel of the Jewish relief organizations here, leaving only native American citizens who are Americans first, last and all the time. As an illustration of what I have in mind I enclose a list giving the names of the members of the Jewish Joint Distribution Committee, from which you will see that twenty-three members of the total of twenty-eight were born outside of the United States, for the most part in Poland and Russia. The question of the American citizenship is not important for they have not for the most part shaken off the prejudices and hatreds of their native country and are thereby unfitted for the duties of a friendly neutral relief worker. I feel exactly the same way about using Polish born Americans of Christian faith on relief work here. They are under similar disadvantages and although we have not had many of them our experience has shown that for work of this sort only well balanced native born Americans should by employed. So long as we go on permitting the employment of foreign born men in American uniforms on this work, so long we must expect to have men who have not been able to conquer their inborn prejudice or the temptation to work against Poland from behind the cover of their American citizenship. This is the more regrettable as there are thousands of American Jews who, I am sure, would gladly offer their services if the need were made clear to them, who would have a proper sense of their responsibility as American citizens and would make it possible for us to help them in a work that should be a source of pride to us. I do not hesitate to say, however, that if the present personnel is left intact and more men of the same sort are sent over, particularly if they are allowed to wear an American uniform, we must be prepared for conflicts, intrigues, and agitation, which will be harmful to our country and to Poland and which will react unfavorably on the situation of the Jews here.

I am, my dear Mr. Secretary,

Very sincerely yours,

Hugh Gibson

Source: Gibson Papers, box 50.

Document No. 7

Gibson speech at the testimonial dinner to Hon. Otto A Rosalsky [12]

New York, June 17, 1920

I am very sorry that since my return to the United States I have not been able to take an active part in the drive conducted by the Joint Distribution Committee. Knowing its work as I do, I was naturally anxious to help maintain and increase its scope but circumstances have rendered it impossible for me to be present when my services could be utilized. I am glad, however, that I am at least privileged to be present at this celebration of the successful outcome of the campaign, and to join in the tribute which is so gladly offered to Judge Rosalsky.

It is a great achievement to have carried through a drive of this sort at a time when there are so many demands on every one and when generosity has been subjected to such a long continued and exacting strain. Judge Rosalsky and his associates have carried through a great campaign in a way that does credit to everybody concerned and we can offer them our wholehearted congratulations on their success.

But to my mind they have done something far better than raising a great sum of money. With recollections of Eastern Europe still fresh in my mind, I cannot but interpret this work in terms of sickness, starvation and suffering of every sort which can now be relieved. I must think of it in terms of families submerged in hopelessness, who for the first time in years can discern the bright promise of a happier future. The total of this work in human happiness cannot be measured by the sums involved, and if there is anything on earth that could repay a man for the hardest sort of work, it is the knowledge that he has been instrumental in bringing happiness and renewed hope into thousands of despairing home. That knowledge Judge Rosalsky has in overflowing measure.

I know that Judge Rosalsky would be the first to deny that he has done this work alone, and that he is the first to give full credit to his associates. But he typifies for us the spirit, the ability, and the energy which have made this campaign possible. We gladly recognize the splendid services of his associates, for the satisfaction to be derived from such good work as can be shared by all the workers without diminishing the share of anyone.

I have been asked to tell you something about conditions in Eastern Europe since the armistice. While I have been pretty well all over those countries in the last year and a half, you will perhaps forgive me if I speak more particularly of Poland as I have watched conditions there for a longer period and in most essential particulars the situation in Poland may be considered as typical. It is not altogether a cheerful story. The present is filled with misery and poverty and suffering. The future doubtless holds much of discouragement and much of sorrow, but I am convinced that in regard to vital questions the future will tend steadily toward better things and that our help can be made to count for much in bringing peace and happiness to that distracted part of the world.

The problems of Eastern Europe are complex, delicate and filled with dangerous possibilities. I don't for a minute believe that we or anybody else can step in and solve these questions off-hand. There is no panacea to cure such ills. Their foundations lie too deep in the past. And if we would work to good effect we must never for a minute forget the past, for therein lies the only true understanding of the present and its problems. The old order has left us a sorry heritage, the result of its corruption and oppression and vicious governmental expedients. The old regime sowed the wind and we are reaping the whirlwind.

To make clear what I have in mind let us go back a little to the time when the three great empires that are now destroyed used as a method of government the policy of sowing hatred and antagonism between different elements of the population, and when the greatest empire of them all, by a fiendishly cold-blooded process, drove millions of its Jews into a narow area where under the restrictions imposed upon them it was desperately hard to keep body and soul together. All of the peoples were consistently and ingeniously led to hate one another — Poles and Lithuanians, White [i.e.Byleo] Russians and Ruthenians, Czechs and Magyars [i.e. Hungarians], and all the others — and each of these to hate the Jews.

But this system was well balanced. For while on the one hand hatreds and prejudices were kept alive to prevent these people from banding together for their own good, still the governments constituted a force such as it was for the maintenance of public order, so that save when it suited the purposes of government, the authorities were able to prevent the actual outbreak of violence and to protect life and property.

Then at the end of the war these great empires crumbled. All these carefully nurtured hatreds were unleashed. There was no constituted authority to maintain order. The lawless elements in many places got control, and the pent-up feelings of centuries found expression in violence.

The worst phase of this passed quickly, but the resentment and prejudice engendered over a long period cannot die out from one day to another, and will go on smoldering for a long time to come. Suspicion and dislike, not only between Jews and Christians, but between different nationalities, can be worn down only by the lapse of time, by intelligent hard work, by common sense, and by unending patience. The world is not going to be an easy place to live in until a better understanding is arrived at among the varied populations of Eastern Europe. When that understanding is reached and such good relations established as ordinary human beings are capable of, we shall have gone a long way to insure the maintenance of peace and prosperity in that part of the world. So the elimination of friction is one of the most important and pressing tasks of constructive statesmanship.

When our people went into Poland and neighboring countries after the armistice, they found a situation that beggars description. Although you are all more or less familiar with it, I should like to touch on its outstanding features.

As regards Poland, they found a country widely devastated, stripped of raw materials, machinery and livestock — a country without a firmly established government, a railway system almost at the point of complete collapse, a food shortage that in many districts amounted to general starvation. There was an epidemic of typhus which had been raging for four years and growing steadily worse each year, warfare, more or less pronounced, was raging on every frontier, and finally, a people so worn by years of suffering that they might be expected to turn in despair to Bolshevism or any other political patent medicine that promised them relief. These are only part of the problems but they constituted a situation that seemed just about hopeless.

And now I ask you to consider the contrast of what we find today.

The devastated regions are being reclaimed and got back to productive normal life. The Government is gaining in autthority and in the ability to maintain order and respect for law. The railway system is rapidly improving in efficiency to meet the demands of normal business. The food situation has passed its most critical state and before long we may expect Poland to be once more at least self-supporting. The anti-

-typhus campaign is being conducted effectively by a mission under Colonel Gilchrist of the [U.S.] Army Medical Corps, with the cordial cooperation of all the American relief organizations. There is no fighting on any front except against the Bolshevisks [sic]. And most important of all there is steadily growing confidence in orderly processes of government as opposed to the cure-alls that are offered by radicals and reactionaries.

This means that the crisis is just about passed. I don't mean to say that our little handful of a few hundred Americans have wrought all these marvels. But they certainly have contributed largely to making possible the rehabilitation of Poland and neighboring countries, and reducing the sum total of human misery to an extent that few of us quite realize. And more important still they have made it possible for us to attack the big constructive work of building a new order as distinguished from the emergency work of fighting for millions of lives. For I am confident that we shall not take our hand from this work until we have made secure the gains already achieved and put these people in a position to work out their own fate.

It is a task so immense that we may by inclined to feel that all our efforts cannot prevail against the many difficulties that tower over us, but I feel strongly that we can do a great deal to solve these problems. I may appear unduly optimistic but I am trying to estimate the possibilities of the future from results already achieved by just this sort of work. I should not be so positive except for the events of the past year in Poland, but I have seen intelligent relief work going on and have been able to gauge its results with some measure of accuracy. I know the tools we have to work with. As you know, we have a large number of organizations working in Poland. Aside from the one in which you are most interested, we have the European Children's Fund, which feeds 1,300,000 children every day and undertakes other activities on a large scale; the American Red Cross, which has an American personnel of about 250, and carries on its work through the country; the anti-Typhus Mission, with a personnel of several hundred Americans; the Y.M.C.A.; the Y.W.C.A.; the National Lutheran Council, and other bodies all of which work in the most complete harmony and are securing a maximum of result for the money and effort expended.

Throughout this time I have been in daily contact with the representatives of the Joint Distribution Committee. I have seen its operations from every angle, have known its difficulties, its discouragements, and the rewards of its work. My relations have been chiefly with Dr. Bogen and Dr. Hirschfield, one or the other whom has been in charge of the work all the time since I went to Poland. No one outside the Committee has had the same opportunity I have had of knowing the difficulty and delicacy of their tasks, or appreciating how steady and patient and hard-working and farsighted they have been. It has been up-hill work from the beginning, but both these men have built up for themselves a position that is a great power good and one that we should all be proud of as Americans. It has been no small triumph for an American Jew to come into the atmosphere of Eastern Europe at a time of such high emotional stress and in a few months command the confidence possessed by these two men. They have not gone in for the tea-party side of the relief work, they are not self-advertised, they do not narrowly stick to their own carefully mapped-out work, but have shown at all times a broad American outlook, a sense of cooperation and a desire to help in any work of general good regardless of race or creed. I am frank to say that Dr. Bogen and Dr. Hirschfield have built up a tradition which does us credit, — one which it is up to us to maintain. Our diplomatic representatives, while they represent our country, are in the nature of things limited in their activities. It is our duty to promote in every possible way the friendships of governments and peoples. We should, of course, to that end utilize every possible instrument. I have traveled throughout the length and breadth of Poland, with Dr. Bogen, and have gone with him into the slums of the bigger cities, and I know what I am talking about when I say that he takes right into the homes of the common people of Poland a real understanding of America, of what America stands for, and of our willingness to share with them the benefits that have been showered upon us. He takes the message of America to people who would never learn it in any other way. The work of such men as I have mentioned is worth more in promoting friendship and good understanding than all the after-dinner speeches and hands-across--the-sea talk that we can do. His work is a positive national asset and he can quite accurately be classed as a missionary of practical Americanism. If we had enough Dr. Bogens in Eastern Europe, we could soon liquidate the so-called Jewish question and never hear of it again save in the past tense.

But the work of all our relief agencies is far from finished. To stop now would be to invite disaster and after what we have put into the work we cannot afford to abandon it. From now on it is going to be a very slow uphill battle with disease and poverty, ignorance and prejudice. It will be an occupation for some hundreds of devoted people who are willing to exist amid sordid surroundings for no reward beyond the mere knowledge that they are playing part in a great game. There will be nothing easy about their lives. It will be one pitiful miserable case after another, of the sort that discourage and distress, but somebody has got to go through with it, and I think our people have the stuff in them that is needed for it.

And this brings us back again to the Joint Distribution Committee which is doing not only emergency work to keep people alive through a crisis, but vital constructive work which goes to the heart of our problem. For the essence of the problem is not diplomatic or political. There is nothing very thrilling about it. It is made up of such humdrum things as food and clothes and medicines and raw materials and above all in providing an opportunity to work in self-respecting occupations. These are the things your people are providing.

I have said a good deal about the activities of the Committee but I don't suppose you all realize the extent and character of the work now being done. The Committee distributes among the poor Jewish population large quantities of imported food, clothing and other commodities. These are for the most part supplies that are scare in Poland such as flour, oil, cloth, and medical supplies. These things are also furnished where needed to the non-Jewish population, and it is a matter of frequent comment in Poland that the policy of your representatives is one of generosity and broad humanity which seeks above all to relieve suffering wherever it is found. We always know where to turn when we are in a tight place. Funds are given in large amounts as subventions to local agencies doing relief among the Jews, — to children's homes, soup kitchens, medical stations, etc., so that the needs of the people may be met as far as possible through their own organizations. Special work is being done for the undernourished children and plans were being made when I left to provide summer colonies where 50,000 such children might have one month of good food and skilled care. In Warsaw alone are 16 stations where some 30,000 children get a glass of milk every day, and you don't know what the certainty of a glass of milk each day means to those half-famished youngsters. There is a training school for nurses supported by the Committee. Much is being done to rehabilitate families on a self-supporting basis against the time when American relief funds are no longer available, by furnishing tools, raw materials or working capital, and by erecting portable houses where they are most needed. It is the aim of the Committee to assist in the rehabilitation of the people by granting loans, by subventions to consumers and producers cooperatives and by helping technical schools, farm colonies, and other agencies working for the development of productive activity among the Jewish population.

This summary is, of course, incomplete but is reveals a vast field of accomplishment. It is sane, sound work that commands universal respect and is doing more for the betterment of relations between the races of Eastern Europe than can be done by any other method.

Dr. Hirschfield was wont to remark with great frequency when people tried to get him off general relief measures with the temptation that comes to all of us to consume our time on individual cases: "We must remember that we are wholesale dealers in poverty." The need for doing work in this impersonal general way is calculated to make one lose sight of the individual, and although all our efforts are expended upon relief, we are every now and then shocked by being brought face to face with the human details of some special case.

To show what I mean I should like to read some extracts from a letter I have just received from Warsaw, citing a couple of typical cases of the sort that must be singled out for some special attention:

"A few days ago a woman came into the office — I recognized her as one whom we had helped several months ago in the form of clothes for her four children. Since we have seen her she has lost two children, — and she came to us for help. She had no money with which to bury the last child, and it had been in the room for a week. She asked for 250 marks for a coffin. We went out to verify the story. Found them in the most pitiful hole. One room, no furniture, and the dead baby on the floor along side of the living ones. The mother was a widow, could find no work, and lived in a village where there was no ECF kitchen. I gave her a thousand marks from our fund, — which gave her a new lease on life."

"Another family had nine children under eleven, All, including the mother and father had had typhus. The mother and father were still in the hospital, and I found the nine kiddies all huddled in their room, cold and practically starving. They had been afraid to go out, and had never heard of the ECF kitchens. I sent them to the nearest kitchen, and laid in a supply of wood and potatoes so that they could exist until the mother returned. The little ten year old girl was a good potato cooker. The youngsters told me that their father had been a house-painter, but that since his illness they had not had a cent of money. Now it seems that the typhus has left the father insane. I will keep an eye on the outfit, and they will benefit further from our fund."

In the face of such things as this, we cannot sit unconcerned. It is such cases as these multiplied many thousand-fold that you are helping today and that we must go on helping till the people can find themselves. Judge Rosalsky must not feel that he has been working in mere sums of money. He has been dealing in far bigger things, the biggest things a man is privileged to touch, in human lives and hearts and hopes. He has brought pulsing life back to a dying people and living courage to those who were sinking in despond. The greatest happiness this life offers is the knowledge that out [sic] efforts have borne such fruit as this. And in the reawakened hopes of these countless people, Judge Rosalsky should find a reward such as come to few among us.

Source: Gibson Papers, box 37.

Document No. 8

Report, Gibson to the Secretary of State [Charles E. Hughes]

No. 1382

Warsaw, November 10, 1922

STRICTLY CONFIDENTAL
FOR THE SECRETARY AND UNDERSECRETARY.

The Honorable
The Secretary of State,
Washington, D.C.

Sir:

On September 23rd the Department telegraphed (Telegraphic Instruction No. 146) asking me for reports on pogroms in Poland. This was
the first time that the question had arisen for over three years but since
replying to the Department's Instruction in my despatch No. 1276 of
September 25th, the subject has come up on several occasions, — always
from American Jewish sources.

I have been approached by a number of Jews with alarming stories
of what happened and what is going to happen. In view of the fact that
these stories may continue and may be brought to the attention of the
Department, I feel that I should report concerning them and their foundation in order that the Department may be in a position to judge as to
the amount of consideration to be given them.

As an example I will take a call which I received on September 28th
from Dr. S. M. Schmidt and Dr. J. J. Golub, who were at the head of the
Joint Distribution Committee work in Poland. They said that they were
very apprehensive as to anti-Jewish excesses during the period of the

coming elections and thought that I should give the matter urgent consideration with a view to seeing what could be done to prevent needless suffering among the Jews. They said that violence had already broken out against the Jews and that this was merely a foretaste of what was coming. I asked them for a statement of any excesses which had already occurred, saying that I had already received inquiries on the subject and was anxious to know exactly what had happened. Dr. Schmidt then alluded to the disorders which I have already reported. I asked him if it were not true that these disorders were less in the nature of a pogrom that of a general protest against the high cost of living and against the swarms of profiteers who were responsible for it. He said that this was perhaps true but that "it was curious that Jews always seemed to get hurt in any protest against the high cost of living."

Dr. Schmidt then turned to what he considered a better case which had occurred during the month of September. He said that a crowd in Kattowitz [Katowice] had attacked and plundered food shops in a given street and that the police had not interfered effectively; that the Polish authorities had tacitly admitted that there had been a pogrom because they were now taking disciplinary action against the police for not controlling the mob. I asked Dr. Schmidt if it were not true that by far the greater part of the shops, at least 75 per cent, were non-Jewish, so that the disorder was clearly a food riot rather than a pogrom. Dr. Schmidt said that this might be the case "if one cared to look at it in that way", but that he did not feel that there was any justification in hurting one Jew just because ten Christians were hurt at the same time.

Dr. Schmidt then went on to say that this was not purely a Polish matter as an American citizen had been seriously injured by the crowds at Kattowitz [Katowice]. This interested me in view of the Department's telegraphic instruction above referred to, and I asked if he had in mind the case of Oscar Haas. Dr. Schmidt stated that Oscar Haas was the man he had in mind, and in reply to further questions he stated that he had full information as to exactly what had happened; that Haas was standing on a street corner when a crowd came along and beat him so severely that he had to be taken to the hospital; that he had since left and gone to Vienna to make a protest to the American Minister. After he had described the incident to me in some detail, I asked him to make me a memorandum on the subject with an exact statement as to his source of information. I then learned that his information on the subject had been acquired from reading the Paris Edition of the CHICAGO TRIBUNE.

All the foregoing may appear frivolous, but I have cited it deliberately as a typical example of the reports which are brought to the Legation in regard to pogroms. A great part of these reports emanate from representatives of the Joint Distribution Committee. They are sent to the New Pork headquarters of the Committee for purposes of publication, propaganda and occasion representations to the Department. In view of this I have thought it well to describe this conversation in some detail in order that the Department might form an opinion as to just how little sense of evidence is to be found among the more responsible leaders of the American Jewish movement. These men have reported the incidents above referred to as established cases of anti--Jewish excesses, and from previous experience, I have no doubt that in case it is considered desirable to make representations to the Department it will be stated as an established fact that pogroms have taken place in Kattowitz [Katowice] on two occasions when the most cursory examination shows that these were food riots in which a small number of Jews were injured along with a larger number of other merchants. According to Dr. Schmidt's own statement he had reported to the New York office of his Committee the serious injury of Oscar Haas, whom he had never seen and of whose treatment he knew nothing except what he had read in the Paris edition of the CHIGAGO TRIBUNE, which is notorious in this part of the world for the complete unreliability of its news service.

In conclusion Dr. Schmidt urged me to keep in touch with Dr. [Isaac] Grünbaum [13], a deputy in the Diet and President of the "National Path" who he said was "gathering information about the excesses which were going to occur". In this connection it is worth noting that the elections passed off quietly and that inquiry from Jewish sources fails to elicit a single instance of mistreatment of Jews.

The American Jewish Committee is apparently at some pains to gather all possible reports, without regard to their accuracy, referring to the mistreatment of Jews. This committee publishes a Monthly Review called A SUMMARY OF EVENTS OF JEWISH INTEREST, which is a compilation of references to printed reports and statements of correspondents (anonymous) as to matters affecting Jews throughout the world, — chiefly grievances, under such headings as "Anti-Semitism, Discrimination, Excesses, Pogroms, Minority Rights, et cetera". A large amount of labor and money must be devoted to compiling this publication and its purpose is a matter of consideration.

In general it can be said that for purposes of agitation these Jewish leaders have a tendency to accept as proof positive any allegations made by a Jew against the Poles and to accept any newspaper report or anonymous statement so long as it indicates that a Jew has been unfairly treated. When these people come to the Legation they expect me to accept as evidence any unsupported story they bring about the mistreatment of Jews and resent any disposition I may show to examine the evidence and verify the facts. This is not said impetuously but as the result of several years of daily dealings with these people. I have encountered this resentment repeatedly, as for instance, when Mr. Lewis [should be Louis] Marshall, Chairman of the American Jewish Committee, issued a scurrilous attack upon me in the press with a number of completely false statements as to what I had said in a confidential report to the Department which has not been published, which he had not even seen and which he did not even ask to see before assuming the responsibility for making a newspaper attack upon me. When I discussed the matter with him in Paris he seemed to feel that he was completely justified in his action by the fact that he had received telegrams from America saying that I had made reports to the Department indicating that there had been no pogroms and that "these reports were causing great harm to Jewish propaganda". I may add that although Mr. Marshall was obliged to admit the falsity of his statements in the presence of several witnesses, he did not consider it necessary to make any amends, and has allowed his misstatements to stand to this day.

While I am quite willing to do anything that may be proper to prevent injustices to the Jews of Poland, I do feel that the time has come when the Department should consider this whole general problem before it arises in an acute form, when it may be difficult to give it the sort of consideration which our national interests require.

As matters now stand there is an avowed disposition on the part of Jewish leaders here and their American Jewish friends, to use the threat of American intervention as a political weapon. Whenever a question arises in the Diet as to Jewish-rights and privileges or Jewish dislikes for pending legislation, the threat is made that is made that unless the Government conforms to Jewish wishes pressure will be brought to bear on the American Government and American pressure in turn brought to bear on Poland.

I have carefully studied the Jewish question in Poland during the time I have been here and am convinced that our intervention on behalf of the Jews can do them nothing but harm. The organized Jews of this country are deliberately and openly anti-Polish. The Jewish press daily hurl abuse at the Polish Government and people and calls down upon them every imaginable curse. The daily run of Jewish callers at the Legation and Consulate General are loud in their denunciations of Poland, its Government and people, and frequently express annoyance if their sentiments do not elicit approval from American representatives.

To begin with, the question arises as to how far the treatment of Jews in Poland is a matter of legitimate interest to the United States. Despite all the agitation by the American Jewish Committee, the Joint Distribution Committee, et cetera, and repeated stories of Jewish massacres in Poland, it was established by Mr. [Henry] Morgenthau that the number of Jews killed in Poland during 1919 was less than the number of negroes killed in the United States during the same period. It must be borne in mind that these excesses occurred in Poland immediately after the collapse of the three Empires which had held this country in subjection, when all restraints were withdrawn and all hatreds and prejudices were unleashed. The excesses in the United States occurred during a time of peace, with none of the excuses to be found here. Yet I am confident that there would have been an outcry from one end of our country to the other if European Governments had suggested sending a commission to investigate the killing of negroes, setting up tribunals to hear their grievances, questioning American officials as to whether they had or had not done their best to prevent disorders, and publishing official reports passing judgment on the conduct of the Government.

It will be remembered that the Powers imposed upon Poland a treaty affording special treatment to Jewish minorities, and that the League of Nations has a legal, if not justifiable, interest in seeing to the enforcement of the Minorities Treaty. I cannot see that our intervention will help the Jews of Poland but I can see many ways in which it will harm our national interests.

I am particularly anxious that we consider this whole question now, not so much because of the possible effect of our interfering in Polish affairs, but because within a few years at most the question will probably arise in a greatly aggravated and magnified form in connection with Russia, and whatever steps we take now will establish a precedent which will either help or hinder us at that time.

Regardless of the denials of Jewish leaders throughout the world, there is a strong conviction in the minds of the common people here and in Russia that the Soviet regime is in the hands of the Jews, and that their oppression is Jewish oppression, — and this is universally resented. Practically everybody who comes out of Russia predicts that when the present restraints are removed there will be a massacre of Jews on a scale unprecedented in modern times. If we begin intervening in Poland at this time, even in a mild way, we shall have established a precedent which will enable the Jewish leaders to bring pressure to bear upon the Department and upon Congress to go into Russia even more energetically and actively for the protection of the Jews, and quite aside from the fact that our efforts would probably be ineffectual, in view of the chaos will exist in Russia for many years, such interference might well jeopardize our national interests without any compensating advantage to the Jews.

I feel very strongly that the whole influence of our Government should be used to secure just treatment for an A m e r i c a n Jew whenever our help is needed, but I feel that there is some question as to how readily our Government should end its influence in behalf of any native element in a foreign country except to prevent gross injustice and cruelty, as in the case of Armenian massacres [14] and the like.

It must be remembered that the Jews here do not demand equal but exceptional treatment. They demand exemption from military service, exemption from certain taxes, separate courts in which cases are to be tried by Jewish law, and separate schools at government expense controlled entirely by themselves at which all subjects will be taught in Hebrew or Yiddish. In order to obtain these demands they resort to any tactics which will place the Poles in an unfavorable position. There is not only no cooperation on their part to build up a Polish State but they endeavor to frustrate the settlement of Polish problems by interference, threats and non-participation. It is clear, therefore, that when these Jewish demands are pressed and the intervention of the United States called for it is not to prevent cruelties and injustices to an oppressed minority but to secure the aid of a large power for their selfish ends in a matter which is a purely internal problem of a friendly State.

For these reasons I venture to suggest that careful consideration be given to the attitude to be adopted toward the treatment of Jews in Poland so that the Department may not be taken unaware by sudden demands for intervention and may be able to adopt a course entirely in harmony with our national interests.

I have the honor to be, Sir,

Your obedient servant,

Hugh Gibson

Source: Gibson Papers, box 100.

NOTES

PREFACE

[1] Gibson to Wilson, March 25, 1919, in: Hugh Gibson Papers, Hoover Institution on War, Revolution and Peace, Stanford, California (hereafter Gibson Papers), box 91.

[2] Gibson diary, April 15, 1919. Gibson Papers, box 70. The Gibson diary was written in the form of daily tellers to his mother, titled "Dearest".

[3] Ibid.

[4] See newspaper clippings in Gibson Papers, box 128.

[5] Eugene C. Black, "Lucien Wolf and the Making of Poland: Paris 1919", *Polin*, 2 (1987), p. 25.

[6] Ronald E. Swerczek, "The Diplomatic Career of Hugh Gibson 1908—1938" (Ph. D. diss., University of Iowa, 1972), pp. 133—4.

[7] Piotr S. Wandycz, *The United States and Poland*, Cambridge, Mass: Harvard University Press, 1980, p. 165.

[8] Kay Lundgreen-Nielsen, *The Polish Problem at the Paris Peace Conference*, Odense: University Press, 1979, p. 375.

1. DURING THE PARIS PEACE CONFERENCE

[1] Norman Davies, *Heart of Europe. A Short History of Poland*, Oxford: Clarendon Press.

[2] A few studies should be singled out for comprehensive description of the Polish-Jewish relations at that time and the proceedings of the Paris Peace Conference with special references to American-Polish-Jewish issues. See: Joseph Marcus, *Social and Political History of the Jews in Poland. 1919—1939*, New York: Mounton Publ., 1983; Wandycz, *The United States and Poland*; Lundgreen-Nielsen, *The Polish Problem*; Arthur Walworth, *Wilson and His Peacemarkers. American Diplomacy at the Paris Peace Conference*, 1919, New York: W. W. Norton and Co., 1986.

[3] Tadeusz Radzik, *Stosunki polsko-żydowskie w Stanach Zjednoczonych Ameryki w latach 1918—1921* [Polish-Jewish Relations in the United States in the Years 1919—1921], Lublin, Polonia Publ., 1988, p. 47.

[4] Wolf Dairy, May 22, 1919. See: Zosa Szajkowski, *Jews, War and Communism*, vol. 2, New York: Ktav Publishing House, 1974, p. 263.

[5] *New York Times*, May 22, 1919, p. 1.

[6] Ibid.

[7] Wandycz, *The United States and Poland*, p. 165.

[8] Andrzej Kapiszewski, „Stosunki polsko-żydowskie w Stanach Zjednoczonych Ameryki" [Polish-Jewish Relations in the United States], in: *Polonia amerykańska. Przeszłość and współczesność*, Tadeusz Gromada, Hieronim Kubiak, Eugeniusz Kusielewicz, eds., Cracow: Ossolineum Publ., 1988, pp. 609—671; Radzik, *Stosunki polsko-żydowskie*, pp. 22—60.

[9] *New York Times*, May 22, 1919, p. 4.

[10] Kapiszewski, *Stosunki polsko-żydowskie*, pp. 628—32, Radzik, *Stosunki polsko-żydowskie*, pp. 52—60.

[11] *Dziennik Związkowy* (Chicago), June 24, 1919, p. 1.

[12] S. Res. 41, *Congressional Record, 66th Congress, Ist Session, 1919*, p. 246.

[13] Ibid., pp. 382, 383, 433, 548.

[14] *Dziennik Polski* (Detroit), June 3, 1919, p. 1. See also Polk to Kleczka, June 11, 1919, *Records of the U.S. Department of State Relating to the Internal Affairs of Poland 1916—1934*, on microfilm, Decimal File 860c., roll 15 (hereafter *Records of the Department of State-Poland*).

[15] Radzik, *Stosunki polsko-żydowskie*, p. 56.

[16] Phillips to Gibson, April 25, 1919, *Papers Relating to the United States, 1919*, vol. 2, Washington: The Department of State, 1934, (hereafter *FR*), p. 748.

[17] Gibson to Phillips, May 17, 1919, *FR*, p. 748.

[18] Polk to Gibson, May 21, 1919, *FR*, p. 749.

[19] Polk to Gibson, May 23, 1919, *FR*, p. 749.

[20] *New York Times*, May 27, 1919, p. 1. Marshall was much concerned with the fate of the Jews in Poland. In the fall of 1918, he held talks with Paderewski and Dmowski in New York. The discussions with Dmowski brought him to the conclusion that Polish nationalists had created serious threat to the future of the Jews in the country. The pogrom in Lvov in November 1918 only reinforced this fear. George J. Lerski, "Dmowski, Paderewski and American Jews", *Polin*, 1987, vol. 2, pp. 95—116.

[21] Ibid., p. 750.

[22] Gibson diary, May 29, 1919, Gibson Papers, box 69.

[23] Gibson to Polk, May 30, 1919, *FR*, p. 750.

[24] *FR*, p. 751.

[25] Gibson to Polk, May 31, 1919, *FR*, pp. 751—52.

[26] Gibson diary, May 30, 1919, Gibson Papers, box 70.

[27] Ibid.

[28] Gibson to Polk, May 31, 1919, *FR*, p. 754.

[29] Ibid.

[30] Gibson to Polk, June 1, 1919, *FR*, p. 755.

[31] Ibid. On June 12 Gibson sent to Washington a joint report made by representatives of the American, British and French Legations in Warsaw about the outbreaks in Częstochowa who reached the conclusion that "all ideas of a premeditated organized pogrom must be dismissed". Gibson to Polk, June 12, 1919, *Department of State-Poland*. On June 14 Gibson cabled also to the Secretary of State the individual testimonies taken by the American members of the Interallied Delegation which investigated the situation in Częstochowa. Ibid.

[32] Gibson to Polk, June 3, 1919, *FR*, pp. 757—760.

[33] Gibson's comment about the existing perception that the United States stood as the advocate of Jews against Poland became widely reported in American newspapers after Phillips quoted it at the House Foreign Affairs Committee hearings. See newspaper clippings, Gibson Papers, box. 128.

[34] Ibid.

[35] Phillips to Gibson, June 3, 1919, *FR*, p. 760.

[36] Gibson to Polk, June 8, 1919, *FR*, pp. 760—61.

[37] *New York Times*, June 11, 1919, p. 3.

[38] Phillips to Gibson, July 29, 1919, Gibson Papers, box 92.

[39] Phillips to Gibson, June 6, 1919, ibid.

[40] It is interesting to note, that the *New York Times* report about outbreaks in Vilna was presented at length in two columns as a main story while information about four pogroms in Russia at the same time in which 29,350 Jews were killed was presented only in a few lines at the bottom of a page. Such disproportionate attention paid to events in Poland in contrast to other places, a common pattern, caused additional tensions within the Polish community.

[41] Polk to Gibson, June 10, 1919, *FR*, p. 761.

[42] Gibson to Polk, June 15, 1919, *FR*, p. 763—64.

[43] Gibson diary, June 13, 1919, p. 3, Gibson Papers, box 70.

[44] Gibson to Polk, June 12, 1919, *FR*, p. 762.

[45] Gibson to the Secretary of State, June 18, 1919, *Department of State-Poland*.

[46] Quote in Zosa Szajkowski, "Western Jewish Aid and Intercession for Polish Jewry 1919—1939", in: *Studies on Polish Jewry 1919—1939*, Joshua A. Fishman, ed., New York: YIVO Institute for Jewish Research, 1974, p. 152.

[47] *New York Times*, June 17, 1919, p. 7.

[48] Pogroms in Pinsk and Lvov are discussed, for example, in Jerzy Tomaszewski, "Lwów, 22 listopada 1918", *Przegląd Historyczny*, 1984, 2, pp. 279—85 and "Pinsk, Saturday 5 April 1919", *Polin*, 1986, pp. 227—51.

[49] Radzik, *Stosunki polsko-żydowskie*, p. 51.

[50] Ibid., p. 52.

[51] Ibid., p. 53.

[52] Gibson to Polk, June 17, 1919, *FR*, pp. 765—68.

[53] Polk to Gibson, June 20, 1919, *FR*, p. 768.

[54] Gibson to Polk, June 25, 1919, *FR*, p. 769.

[55] Polk to the Senate, June 26, 1919, *FR*, p. 770.

[56] Gibson to Dolbeare, June 26, 1919, Gibson Papers, box 92. See also Gibson to Lippman, August 9, 1919, Gibson Papers, box 43.

[57] Gibson diary, June 24, 1919, Gibson Papers, box 70.

[58] Lansing to the Secretary of State, June 26, 1919, *Department of State-Poland*.

[59] Phillips to Lansing, June 28, 1919, *FR*, p. 771.

[60] Ibid., p. 772.

[61] Polk to Lansing, June 23, 1919, Gibson Papers, box 92. See also Phillips to Gibson, July 29, 1919, Gibson Papers, box 56.

[62] Gibson to Dolbeare, June 26, 1919, Gibson Papers, box 92. See also House diaries, June 24, 1919, Sterling Library, Yale University, vol. 15, p. 250. The Senate approved Gibson nomination without reservations.

[63] Gibson diary, June 29, 1919, Gibson Papers, box 70.

[64] Marshall to Elkus, August 19, 1919, in: Charles Reznikoff, ed., *Louis Marshall: Champion of Liberty. Selected Papers and Addresses*, Philadelphia: The Publication Society of America, 1957, vol. 2, pp. 10—11.

[65] Gibson diary, June 27, 1919, Gibson Papers, box 70.

[66] Ibid.

[67] Ibid.

[68] Ibid.

[69] Ibid.

[70] Gibson to Phillips, July 6, 1919, Gibson Papers, box 92.

[71] Ibid.

[72] Wheeler to the Secretary of State, July 8, 1919, *Department of State-Poland*.

[73] Marshall to Elkus, August 19, 1919, in: *Louis Marshall, Champion of Liberty*, pp. 1—11.

2. THE MORGENTHAU MISSION

[1] George J. Lerski, *Herbert Hoover and Poland. A Documentary History of a Friendship*, Stanford: Hoover Institution Press, p. 16. Hoover shared the view that Jewish agitation in the United States over the mistreatment of Jews in Poland had been founded "on misinformation" as news from Poland was filtered through German and Bolshevik sources. He also believed that many Jews in Poland did not support the Polish government, were subject to "Bolshevik influence", and were incited by Germans "to make trouble". Hoover to Wilson, June 2, 1919. Ibid., pp. 75—76. According to Szajkowski " Hoover was of the opinion that Polish anti-Semitism was due to some clauses in the Minority Treaties and to Zionism". Szajkowski, *Jews, War and Communism*, p. 262.

[2] Gibson to the Department of State, June, 1919, *FR*, p. 769.

[3] Polk to Lansing, June 26, 1919, *Department of State-Poland.*

[4] Lansing to Polk, July 2, 1919, *FR*, pp. 772—73.

[5] Gibson to the Department of State, July 4, 1919, *Department of State-Poland.*

[6] Ibid.

[7] Gibson to the Department of State, July 9, 1919, *Department of State-Poland.*

[8] Gibson to Harrison, July 7, 1919, Gibson Papers, box 43.

[9] Gibson to Lippman, August 9, 1919, Gibson Papers, box 51. Walter Lippman, well known author, was at that time a staff member of the American delegation to the Paris Peace Conference.

[10] Ibid.

[11] Gibson diary, July 3, 1919, Gibson Papers, box 70.

[12] See newspaper clippings, Gibson Papers, box 128. For example, Herman Bernstein, special correspondent of the *New York Herald, after spending several weeks in Poland, wrote that outbreaks against the Jews were worse than Russian pogroms and that Gibson's reports were based on "superficial, hasty investigation". *New York Herald*, August 3, 1919.

[13] Gibson to the Secretary of State, July 12, 1919, *Department of State-Poland.*

[14] Gibson diary, July 12, 1919, Gibson Papers, box 70.

[15] Lansing to the Department of State, July 13, 1919, *Department of State-Poland.*

[16] Gibson diary, July 17, 1919, Gibson Papers, box 70. See also newspaper clippings, Gibson Papers, box 128. The Jewish accusation against Bogen were also widely reported in Polish-American newspapers.

[17] On Morgenthau's attitude toward Zionism, see his memoirs (written in collaboration with French Strother), *All in a Life-Time*. Garden City, N. Y.; Doubleday, Page and Co., 1922, pp. 348—51. Morgenthau was a representative to the Jewish congress held in Philadelphia in 1918 which was electing members to the Jewish commission to be sent to the Paris Peace Conference to secure assurances in the Peace Treaties of Jewish rights in the countries of Central Europe. As the congress became dominated by Zionists, Morgenthau decided not to attend it, and signed, along with few other Jewidh leaders, a statement against Zionist agitation. These actions brought him into conflict with the Zionist-dominated delegation of American Jews in Paris. Szajkowski suggested, that Wilson choose Morgenthau deliberately "to bring back a report directed against Jewish nationalists", "Western Jewish Aid", p. 152.

[18] Lippmann to Gibson, July 14, 1919, Gibson Papers, box 51.

[19] Gibson to Dolbeare, June 26, 1919, Gibson Papers, box 43. See also Morgenthau diary, June 8, 11 and 12, 1919, Library of Congress.

[20] Morgenthau, *All in a Life-Time*, pp. 354—56.

[21] Phillips to Gibson, July 29, 1919, Gibson Papers, box 56.

[22] Frankfurter wrote in his memoirs: "It was felt that it was important for him

[i.e. Morgenthau] to know that he was being watched, so it was arranged that I should go to Poland". Felix Frankfurter, *Reminiscences,* recorded in talks with Hartlan B. Phillips, New York: Reynal and Co., 1960, p. 160.

[23] Gibson to Grew, July 14, 1919, Gibson Papers, box 43.

[24] Gibson to Harrison, July 8, 1919, Gibson Papers, box 43, See also Harrison to Gibson, July 24, 1919, and Gibson to Harrison, August 1, 1919, Gibson Papers, box 43.

[25] Grew to Morgenthau, July 17, 1919, Gibson Papers, box 43.

[26] Gibson to Harrison, August 1, 1919, Gibson Papers, box 43.

[27] Gibson to Grew, July 31, 1919, Gibson Papers, box 43. See also comments in Gibson's diary, July 21, 1919, Gibson Papers, box 70.

[28] Gans to Mackenzie, July 27, 1919, a copy in Gibson Papers, box 43.

[29] Frankfurter, *Reminiscences,* pp. 156—57.

[30] Radzik, *Stosunki polsko-żydowskie,* p. 62.

[31] Lansing, in his letter to Morgenthau, instructed the commission "to make careful inquiry into all matters affecting the relations between the Jewish and non-Jewish element in Poland" for the purpose "of seeking to discover the reason lying behind [anti-Jewish] excesses and discriminations with a view to finding a possible remedy, as the American Government would like "to render service to all elements in the new Poland: Christians and Jews alike", Lansing to Morgenthau, June 30, 1919, *Department of State-Poland.*

[32] Radzik, *Stosunki polsko-żydowskie,* p. 65.

[33] Ibid.

[34] For a detailed description of the mission's activities see notes by a counsel to it: Arthur L. Goodhart, *Poland and the Minority Races,* New York: Brentano's, 1920.

[35] It is worth quoting here Gibson's decription of the comments made to him by Józef Piłsudski about the mission. After greeting Morgenthau and talking with him about the situation in Poland, Piłsudski told Gibson that: "he saw we had had a pogrom in New York and thought it might be necessary for him to send over a Mission to make an inquiry so as to quiet Polish public opinion ... as the darkies had been cutting loose in Washington and the whites retaliating it might be that the negro colony of two or three in Warsaw would demand that something be done to bring our barbarous people to a sense of its responsibilities". Gibson diary, July 27, 1919, Gibson Papers box 70. Piłsudski's comments, though made in a form of a joke, reflected the attitudes of many Poles who felt offended by the fact that the foreign mission was investigating what they perceived as Polish internal affairs, not trusting the results of official inquiries and government statements.

[36] Szajkowski, *Jews, War and Communism,* p. 262.

[37] Ibid.

[38] Gibson diary, July 20, 1920, Gibson Papers box 70.

[39] Gibson to Phillips, August 29, 1919, Gibson Papers, box 56.

[40] Morgenthau to Hoover, August 12, 1919, Gibson Papers, box 91.

[41] Hoover's response to Morgenthau's letter is not known.

[42] Gibson diary, September 16, 1919, Gibson Papers box 70.

[43] Morgenthau to Gibson, January 14, 1920, Gibson Papers, box 54.

[44] U.S. Congress. Senate. S. 177, *Mission of the United States to Poland* (hereafter *Mission to Poland*), 66th Congress, 2nd Session, 1920, p. 13.

[45] Grew to Gibson, October 29, 1919, Gibson Papers, box 43.

[46] Phillips to Gibson, November 25, 1919, Gibson Papers. box 56.

[47] *Mission to Poland,* p. 9.

[48] Morgenthau, *All in a Life-Time,* p. 382.

[49] Ibid., pp. 383—84.

[50] *Mission to Poland,* pp. 13—24.

[51] Ibid.

[52] Today some Jewish historians describe them as a "whitewash of Poland's policies", Szajkowski, *Jews, War and Communism*, p. 262.

[53] See "Why the Jews Dislike the Morgenthau's Report", *The Dearborn Independent*, October 30, 1920.

[54] See the report by Polish Minister in Washington to the Ministry of Foreign Affairs, February 5, 1920, in the collection of the Polish Embassy in Washington (hereafter Polish Emb. Wash.), Hoover Archives, box 66.

[55] Gibson to Phillips, December 29, 1919, Gibson Papers, box 56.

3. THE CONTINUING PROBLEM

[1] Gibson to Harrison, February 14, 1920, Gibson Papers, box 43.

[2] Harrison to Gibson, November 24, 1919, Gibson Papers, box 43.

[3] See, for example, Norman Davies, *White Eagle, Red Star. The Polish-Soviet War, 1919—1920*, London: Macdonald Publ., 1972, p. 328 or Kapiszewski, *Stosunki polsko-żydowskie*, pp. 626—27.

[4] See Radzik, *Stosunki polsko-żydowskie*, p. 75.

[5] Gibson to Lansing, February 14, 1920, Gibson Papers. box 50.

[6] Gibson Papers, box 37.

[7] Gibson to Mary Gibson, June 18, 1920, Gibson Papers, box 37.

[8] Copy at the collection of Polish Emb. Wash., box 66.

[9] Gibson to the Secretary of State, January 12, 1922, Gibson Papers, box 101.

[10] Gibson to Lansing, February 29, 1922, Gibson Papers, box 101.

[11] Gibson to the Secretary of State, November 10, 1922, Gibson Papers, box 100.

[12] Quoted in *Polish Jews*, 1938, p. 154.

DOCUMENTS

[1] So called "Haller troops" refer to the Polish army formed in the end of 1918 and early 1919 in France under the csommand of General Józef Haller. Many soldiers in this army were Polish volunteers from America. In April 1919 Haller's Army arrived in Poland and was sent to the Eastern front.

[2] Louis Marshall was one of the leaders of American Jewish Committee and at that time the influential member of the delegation of American Jews at the Paris Peace Conference.

[3] Felix Frankfurter was an Austrian-born American jurist who represented in Paris the Zionist movement of the U.S.

[4] Jacob Schiff from the American Jewish Committee and Abram Elkus, former US Ambassador in Turkey were highly respected members of the American Jewish community.

[5] Szymon Askenazy was a well known Polish historian and diplomat. In the years 1920—23 he represented Poland in the League of Nations.

[6] Kazimierz Lutosławski was an extreme right wing Polish politician, closely cooperating with Roman Dmowski. He was a member of Polish Parliament since 1919.

[7] William Phillips was at that time an Assistant Secretary of State.

[8] Joseph C. Grew was a Secretary of the American Commission to Negotiate Peace in Paris.

[9] For the description of this meeting see George J. Lerski, "Dmowski, Paderewski and American Jews", *Polin*, 1987, vol. 2, pp. 95—116.

[10] Nahum Sokolov, a Zionist, was the President of the Provisional Jewish National Council of Poland and the chairman of the Committee of Jewish Delegations at the Paris Peace Conference.

[11] Boris Bogen and Isidore Hirschfield were representatives of the American Jewish Joint Distribution Committee in Poland.

[12] Otto A. Rosalsky, judge, was one of the leaders of the Joint Distribution Committee.

[13] Isaac Grünbaum, lawyer, one of the leading Zionists in Poland, was an influential member of Polish Parliament.

[14] Gibson relates to the massacres of the Armenians by Turks and Kurds in the years 1914—19.

INDEX OF NAMES